WHEN GOD BECAME MAN

By

GEORGE L. LAWLOR

MOODY PRESS

CHICAGO

Library of Congress Cataloging in Publication Data

Lawlor, George L
    When God became man.
    Bibliography: p. 150
    1. Jesus Christ—Person and offices. I. Title.

BT202.L39   232   78-15741

ISBN 0-8024-9426-9

To my many students in Greek at
Cedarville College, past and present,
with the earnest prayer that they will
never forget that our blessed Lord
intends them to use the original language
of the New Testament in their ministry
of the Word.

CONTENTS

FOREWORD

More than thirty-five years ago, the author of this treatise, Dr. George L. Lawlor, came to know the Lord Jesus Christ as his personal Savior. Almost immediately the Holy Spirit created in him a desire to serve the Lord in some active and tangible way. At the time, the ministry seemed to him to be where his efforts should be directed. Realizing his need for training in the Scriptures, he applied for entrance to Grace Theological Seminary and was admitted as a special student.

His performance as a student was remarkable in view of his meager background. He took the regular three-year course of study including the biblical languages of Greek and Hebrew. Following graduation, he completed his undergraduate study and was awarded the degree Bachelor of Divinity. Later he pursued the Master of Theology degree, and still later the Doctor of Theology degree, both at Grace Theological Seminary.

He began his work as a pastor and later transferred to the ministry of teaching Bible and New Testament Greek at Cedarville College, where he has done commendable work over these many years. His intense enthusiasm for the study of the Scriptures, especially of the New Testament in the original language, has inspired many students to seek further training in the Word of God and to channel their efforts toward the ministry, missionary service, and Christian teaching.

Early in his study of the Word of God, the kenosis passage of Philippians captured his heart. This became the motivating force in his life and the subject for lifelong study. It has

at last resulted in this treatise, *When God Became Man*. It
will be evident to all who read this exposition that Dr. Lawlor
has poured into this treatment the wealth of many years of
study and, more importantly, his whole mind, soul, and body.

There is no doubt in the minds of earnest students of the
Word of God that the focus of all eternity is upon this event
in the life and ministry of Christ so incomparably expressed in
the few brief sentences from the pen of the apostle Paul.
Eternity past looked forward to the Lamb "foreordained before the foundation of the world" (1 Pet. 1:20) and "slain
from the foundation of the world" (Rev. 13:8). And eternity
future will look back to this event and join in exultation and
adoration of the Lamb (Rev. 21:9, 14, 22, 23, 27; 22:1, 3).

The incarnation, propitiation, resurrection, and exaltation
of Christ is the central area of all theology. The plan of God
from all eternity anticipated and provided for the entrance of
His Son into the stream of human history. This plan culminated in the incarnation, death, and subsequent exaltation
of Christ. In that ministry the foundation for the realization
of the Kingdom of God was laid. Any system of eschatology
that dares ignore this ministry incurs the peril of building a
house on shifting sands.

As Dr. Lawlor has so well pointed out, Paul's delineation
of the ministry of Christ was intended for a practical applica-
tion in the lives of the saints. The mind that moved Christ in
every step from glory to earth and return to glory is the mind
that Paul urges saints to cultivate in their lives (2:5). This
must mean that the unfathomable depths of Christology are
practical and can be understood and applied to human life.
It further means that with varying degrees of apprehension,
every saint will find something to challenge him, from the
moment he enters the Christian faith until he is taken home to
be with Christ.

Volumes have been written on this short passage of Scripture, and it has never yet been exhausted. Witness the lengthy

bibliography consulted by Dr. Lawlor. And he would admit that he did not dare list all the volumes he has consulted in the long period of his study. The last word has not yet been spoken on this passage of Scripture, and Dr. Lawlor would be the first to admit that this treatise is not in any sense to be taken as the last word. He has not said all that he would like to say, but wisdom dictates that there is a time to stop.

I count it a high privilege and a real pleasure to write this foreword. I commend this worthy and penetrating exposition to all the saints. Those who read it will catch the spirit of the writer and will find their own souls lifted to higher heights as they behold in larger perspective that ministry which Christ performed in order that they might become members of the family of God. Above all, let those who read this treatise hear echoing and reechoing through the corridors of their minds, "Let this mind be in you, which was also in Christ Jesus" (Phil. 2:5).

HERMAN A. HOYT

PREFACE

Christology lies at the very center of the current theological turmoil in Christendom. Nothing seems more apparent than that there is a great need among the people of God who constitute the local church assemblies for a Christology that is straightforward, accurate, and scriptural in its details. Both clergy and lay people, and in a special sense the young people growing up in the local churches, must have a truly biblical understanding of the person and work of our Lord Jesus Christ, for these are days when the true church is besieged by all kinds of speculative theories and devious ideas concerning this subject.

One of the ways in which this need can be met is by the availability of commentaries, study books, and sources that are neither too unduly technical to be fully understood nor too elementally popular to convince and satisfy the thoughtful. The aim of the writer is to place in the hands of pastors, teachers, students, and readers of the New Testament a study book on the person and work of Christ that will contribute to the supply of this need.

Who really was this Jesus of Nazareth, and what was His mission? Does He actually exist today? If so, who is He, what is He, where is He? Many modern theologians answer these questions by stating that He was simply a great teacher and miracle worker who possessed more God-consciousness than any other man and who saw Himself as the "last herald" before the coming of the Kingdom of God. They write Him off as only an unusual man, who in His lifetime carried out an assignment given to Him by God, but whose death was the end of His existence. His death on the cross is taken to be

9

only the tragic fate of a great man who became a martyr for the message He undertook to proclaim. In fact, in the popular view, the birth, life, ministry, death, and resurrection of Christ actually have no bearing on faith.

Where, then, do the preexistence of Christ, His virgin birth and incarnation, His vicarious death on the cross, His bodily resurrection, and His physical ascension in glory come in? Are they literally true? What do they mean? How are they to be understood? How are they to be received and interpreted by the church? This book is an attempt to answer these questions. It is written for believers in general, for all Christians who are genuinely concerned about widespread departure from the truth of the Bible.

It is also a study book on one of the great Christological passages of the New Testament, where all these great facts concerning Christ appear, both by deliberate mention and by obvious inference. The author seeks to stir the minds and hearts of believers to the grandeur of what is perhaps the most sublime paragraph in the Holy Scriptures, Philippians 2:5-11, where the truth concerning the blessed person and redemptive work of our Lord Jesus Christ is set forth. The passage, in itself, is not a controversial assertion but a great doctrinal appeal to the heart and life.

The author has also attempted to refute current theological fadism that would dismiss Christian doctrine in favor of Christian humanitarianism. Christian doctrine is the articulate statement of eternal and vital facts in the Holy Scriptures to the end that we shall live by them.

Finally, this book is written in order that Christian believers, tempted daily to a life of self-assertion, may look not on their own things but, in lowliness of mind, esteem others better than themselves.

The book is based on the King James Version (KJV), because this is the version a majority of believers possess and use, and it should not necessarily be shunted aside in favor of the modern speech versions. Scripture quotations are from the Scofield edition (1967) of the King James Version or from the original Greek text. The Greek text has been used not to confuse or complicate, but as an aid to the study. Greek words which appear in the text have been transliterated into their English-alphabet equivalents to help those readers who are unfamiliar with the Greek language.

INTRODUCTION

The epistle to the Philippians is a masterpiece of doctrine and duty, the great treatise in which normal Christian experience is revealed as based upon, centered in, and patterned after the person and work of Christ. To the church of all ages, and to the church of the present day in particular, this epistle teaches a mighty lesson. It draws us away from everything else to the heart of the gospel: the life of Christ and the life in Christ, in whom doctrine and duty are joined together. The need for the exposition of Philippians in our churches today is great indeed, for this epistle magnificently reveals the meeting point of all our differences, the adjustment of our difficulties, the healing of our feuds, the pattern for our living, the true and normal high experience for Christians and churches alike. All is found in Christ. Whatever living may be for others, for Christians and churches everywhere the sum total of living is Christ. All of our apprehension and experience of Christ and our insight into the great truths concerning Him must be affirmed and embodied in the conduct and conflict of the daily Christian life. Conduct is the true, practical confession of our faith. It is the verification of our experience in Christ. There is no greater, more dangerous operation of unbelief than that which on the one hand does not outwardly question the doctrine but which renders the life cold and careless; or that which on the other hand subtly rejects the doctrine but assumes a form of godliness.

The doctrinal content of Philippians is centered in chapter 2. Yet on every side of the great doctrinal passage in 2:5-11, duty is clearly set forth. In perhaps no other single chapter of the New Testament are doctrine and duty so closely and remarkably joined.

The apostle arrives at this place in the epistle over a course that may be followed with gratifying ease of understanding. After his opening salutation and thanksgiving in 1:1-3, he speaks with great delicacy and intense feeling concerning Christian fellowship. To check the tendency in the Philippian congregation toward a spirit of strife and social rivalry, Paul tactfully hints that he is not a factionist. He offers prayer for all, shows concern for all, looks upon all as copartners in his great cause, makes plain that his heart yearns for them all, and declares that he desires all to be sincere and to bear the fruits of righteousness.

He then speaks of proper attitudes, explaining his own circumstances and showing how they turned to the pioneer advance of the gospel. He wishes them to learn from their circumstances, whether God-ordained or God-permitted, that they must seek the furtherance of the message of Christ. He refers to the rivalry of other preachers, the zeal of his friends, and his own great personal hope, aim, and purpose. Let theirs be the same, and let ours be the same. He summons the attention of his readers to the great purpose of their presence in this world: the help and advantage of others, for someone else's furtherance and joy of faith.

Finally he points out the need for a daily life befitting the gospel, urging all to steadfastness and unity, to "stand fast in one spirit, with one mind striving together for the faith of the gospel" (1:27). From there he moves to the appeal in 2:1-4, in which he presses earnestly upon them the need for a unity of mind and heart that will demonstrate itself among them. This leads him in 2:5-8 to hold out to them and to all believers, for their and our example, the mind of Christ, the Lord of glory, who, supreme above all, nevertheless did not assert His divine majesty and authority but humbled Himself to become the lowliest of the lowly.

The entire paragraph of 2:5-11 is a classic passage, as Lenski says, "a great sedes doctrinae."[1] Although the doctrine is introduced incidentally and strictly employed to enforce Christian practice and holiness of life, nevertheless the passage is a grand statement of the facts, the realities of the Christian faith, which the minds and hearts of all believers are to receive. The passage asserts the distinctive articles of the doctrine of Christ. The apostle, under inspiration, insists upon the preexistence of Christ, His deity, His equality with God the Father, His incarnation, His true humanity, His atoning death upon the cross, His resurrection from the dead (by inference), and His ascension and exaltation in glory.

In our reading of the passage, we must note that verse 5 is transitional, linking the opening appeal to the great facts of verses 6-11. It is most important for us to see that Paul is urging upon the readers the instruction he has just given by bringing them to the supreme example of the Lord Jesus Christ Himself. The setting forth of what Christ was and is, of what He did, and of His present exalted position is for the purpose of exhibiting His mind and His example toward a practical end. But we must remember that the passage is designed to set before the readers not only the example of Christ, but *Christ Himself* and His servanthood, which issued in His death on a cross. Hence, we have here perhaps the greatest Christological passage in the New Testament.[2]

The passage is known as the "kenosis" passage, drawing this name from the Greek verb *kenoō*, which means "to empty,

1. R. C. H. Lenski, *The Interpretation of St. Paul's Epistles to the Galatians, to the Ephesians, and to the Philippians,* p. 775. Lenski adds: "This is doctrine. Although it is used in support of hortation (v. 5), Paul presents pure doctrine, which means a statement of the facts, the realities which the hearts of the readers are to receive."
2. H. C. G. Moule, at the conclusion of his comments on this section, in vv. 5-11, states: "So closes one of the most conspicuous and magnificent of the dogmatic utterances of the New Testament" (*Philippian Studies,* pp. 96-97). See Moule's additional comments on pp. 99-100.

evacuate." The word appears in verse 7 (*ekenōsen*), where it is translated "made himself of no reputation" (KJV) or "emptied Himself" (NASB). His deity was adjusted to His true humanity without giving up the former or reducing the latter.

The adoption of this principle of interpretation with relation to the person of Christ is sound and biblical, because the Scriptures do teach a kenosis of some kind in connection with the doctrine of the incarnation. The great problem lies in the nature of the self-emptying of Christ. Unfortunately, those who have attempted to explain it apart from the supernatural have failed to keep their eyes fixed steadfastly upon the historic person of the Lord Jesus Christ and have not allowed the mind of the Lord to abide in them. Consequently the kenosis has become, as Dr. Alva J. McClain once remarked, "a tool of theological bias, and used for the construction of strange kenotic Christs bearing but a poor and partial resemblance to the Christ of the Gospel records."[3] The fact is that the Christ of the liberal interpretations of the kenosis bears little, if any, resemblance to the virgin-born, incarnate Son of God.

The major difficulty of the incarnation is, of course, the relation of the divine to the human in the historic Jesus Christ. Paul must certainly have been aware of the problem that would be raised by his great Christological statement, yet neither he nor the other New Testament writers make any attempt to solve or explain it.[4] The writers of Holy Scripture are content to state the fact of the two natures in Christ with-

3. From Alva J. McClain's lectures in Systematic Theology, Grace Theological Seminary, Winona Lake, Ind., 1943.
4. It is both important and interesting to note that Paul did not hesitate to make this great theological statement to the members of the local church at Philippi, who were common Christians like ourselves. This sublime Christological passage was given only to the leaders of the church there, nor was it intended solely for the clergy in succeeding generations. It is not alone for discussion and development among theologians, Bible teachers, and gospel preachers, but it is likewise directed to the hearts and minds of all believers, and designed for the blessedness of the whole body of Christian people.

out attempting to render their doctrine conformable to human reason.

In the New Testament Scriptures, Christ is true man, "made of a woman" (Gal 4:4) and a "partaker of flesh and blood" (Heb 2:14), yet we are never permitted to forget that there is a great difference between Him and other men. *We* are sinners, but *He* is "holy, harmless, undefiled, separate from sinners, and made higher than the heavens" (Heb 7:26). Weary in body, He goes to sleep in the bottom of the fishing boat, yet in the next moment, in answer to the cry of the apostles for help, He arises to still the waves of the tumultuous sea. He weeps with profound grief at the grave of His friend Lazarus, and then calls Lazarus out of the darkness and death of the tomb. He is arrested and taken by the officers in the garden; but when He identifies Himself to them as "I am" (*egō eimi*), they are hurled backward and sprawling to the ground. That He is true man, there is no doubt. The evidence is clear; the proofs are many. At the same time, He is true God. Again there is no doubt. Here is the great miracle of the ages: He is "the man Christ Jesus" (1 Tim 2:5), yet He is also nothing less than the One "who is over all, God blessed forever" (Rom 9:5).

It is undoubtedly best to leave the matter where the writers of the Holy Scriptures have left it. Finite minds cannot fully interpret infinite truth, and confusion and controversy have resulted when well-intentioned men have attempted to explain and rationalize the eternal verities and have slipped into damaging errors.

Still, the believing church has been compelled to enter the arena of dissension because of regrettable deviations and departures from Christological doctrine that the Bible writers were moved by the Holy Spirit to record. At the Council of Chalcedon in A.D. 451, a comparatively few theologians dared to stand for the truth, and it was formally declared that our

Lord Jesus Christ possesses two natures, one fully divine and the other fully human. These two natures are perfectly and organically united in one Person, yet remain distinct, each retaining its own complete integrity.

After ensuing centuries of controversy and conflict, it became the responsibility of the Reformation, and particularly the leaders of the Reformed Church, to recall to the minds of men the fact of the real humanity of the preexistent Son of God. At the same time, the Reformers conceded nothing to the Socinian tendencies of their time, but insisted that in becoming true man, the Saviour yielded up no part of His deity. The Reformed theologians did not solve the problem of the two natures in the one person of Christ, but they called the attention and allegiance of theologians and church leaders back to a true biblical Christology that insisted upon the full deity and the full humanity of our Lord Jesus Christ. Moreover, they steadfastly refused to give consideration and credence to any view of His person that failed to assign, in any sense, the proper regard to all the facts concerning the Lord's deity and humanity that are set forth in the New Testament Scriptures.

Today, in this age of mounting apostasy, when theological extremists are flooding Christendom with exaggerated and erroneous views concerning Christ and with false kenotic theories, the believing church has been compelled again to stand up and insist upon a true Christology. When the doctrine of Christ is under persistent and vicious attack, and when the person of Christ is being so critically analyzed by superficial religionists, responsible theologians, and all true Christians—the people of the churches as well as their leaders—must set themselves to calling the church back to the incontrovertible fact of proper deity and true humanity in the one magnificent person of the Lord Jesus Christ. For without doubt, He is the preexistent Son of God, who became incarnate in human flesh, form, and nature, by virgin birth, for the purpose of taking away our sins and rendering inoperative the work of the devil (1 John 3:5, 8).

This indescribable stooping to the form of servanthood is at the heart of the mighty Christological passage in Philippians 2:5-11, and the true kenosis view neither confounds the natures nor divides the person. All that is said here of Jesus Christ is true as it stands, and it has stood through the ages. It is the expression of the great mind and heart of the eternal God. It will never pass away. It is for all true believers, so let us note it well.

TRANSITION

Let this mind be in you, which was also in Christ Jesus (Phil 2:5).

Philippians 2:5-11 is one of the most conspicuous of the great utterances of the New Testament Scriptures. The statement in Philippians 2:5 calls for close attention, since it forms the significant link between verses 1-4 and the section that follows in verses 6-11. The pronoun "this" (*touto*) has an emphatic position in the sentence, which shows its importance and indicates the relationship of the exhortation in verse 5 to that which precedes it. The first clause, "Let this mind be in you," reaches back and connects with verses 1-4, while the second clause, "which was also in Christ Jesus" carries forward to the great illustration in verses 6-11, introduced by the relative pronoun "who" (*hos*). Basically, verses 1-4 set forth the true character of the Christian life and experience, that which must mark the conduct of believers among themselves.[1] The pronoun "this" goes back to the spirit of humility, of self-abnegation, and the sincere interest in the welfare of others taught in the context of verses 1-4. It is this attitude that the apostle speaks of as being the mind of Christ and supremely exemplified in His conduct.[2]

The verb *phroneite* ("let this mind be, be minding") is interesting and has been chosen by the Holy Spirit for our un-

1. S. T. Bloomfield says, "We should understand the verb as disposition, way of thinking and acting. The expression must be especially meant of the disposition here particularly adverted to—humility" (*Philippians*, in *The Greek Testament with English Notes* 2:298).
2. Again Bloomfield comments, "The apostle follows up his precept in 1, 3, 4, by placing before them the greatest example of humility, in Christ Jesus" (Ibid.).

derstanding of this significant statement. It is from the Greek verb *phroneō,* which expresses the action of the mental faculties as well as the heart and will, the thoughts and understanding, all of which are more or less to be found in our verb *to think.* The word might be translated in several ways, each holding mainly to the central idea, yet bringing out slightly different shades of meaning. For example, it is rendered: "Be constantly thinking" (Wuest); "Be intent within yourselves" (Thayer); "Have this mind within you" (Kennedy); and "Reflect in your minds" (Lightfoot). The same Greek word is used in Acts 28:22 as indicative of what one thinks, that is, *opinion;* in Romans 8:5 to express the *directing of one's mind to something;* in Romans 12:3 of *self-estimation;* in 1 Corinthians 13:11 to designate *understanding;* in Philippians 4:2 of *agreement together.* It seems best to take the verb here in its simplest meaning, as "be minding."

The present tense of the verb denotes the fact that the saints are to be constantly directing their minds to the great facts that follow, to continue being intent upon those facts as a habitual course of meditation and action. When the verb is understood as an imperative, it becomes incumbent upon believers to recognize that such a course of thought and action is vital indeed, and must be engaged in and obeyed unflinchingly.

We would do well to pursue further study in connection with this verb in order to acquire as thorough an understanding of its meaning as possible, for it shows the purpose of the example of Christ—an example that we must accept and follow. "Be minding" means minding the things the Lord minded, loving what He loved, hating what He hated. The thoughts, desires, and motives of true Christians should be the thoughts, desires, and motives that filled the sacred heart of our Lord. We must therefore strive to imitate Him, to reproduce His image in both our inner and outer lives. Here we are bidden to follow especially the pattern of His humility and unselfishness. The verb suggests that the great rule of Christian practice is the imitation of Christ—the habitual, daily direction of the mind to the distinctive *virtues* of Christ-likeness.

Beginning with verse 2, one might draw a line from "be like-minded" to "of one mind" in the same verse, then to "lowliness of mind" in verse 3, and finally to "Let this mind be in you" in verse 5. Verses 3 and 4 tell us that what we are to keep minding is having the same love and being joined in soul. Nothing springing from self-seeking should be allowed to motivate our conduct. On the contrary, with due lowliness of mind, our practice is to be that of holding others up above ourselves, considering them more excellent than we are. Paul has already struck the keynote for this teaching in 1:22-26. Each of us is to be watching out not for our own things exclusively, but also for the things of others. "This" we are to be continually minding. It is presented to us as that which was in Christ Jesus and revealed in Him, who is our Model and Example.

So the transition is complete, and the passage from verses 1-4 into the great illustration in verses 6-11 is indeed superb. "This be minding in you, which was also in Christ Jesus." He is the great divine pattern, the Person who has come and gone yet is still with His own. He has marked out the way; we are to follow His steps. It cannot be selfish following. "This be minding" means humility and self-abnegation on our part, for it is the self-emptying of Christ, the humiliation of our Lord, that forms the pattern for us. That pattern is clear. Although existing before the ages in the blessed, eternal Godhead, He did not selfishly and greedily, ambitiously and forcibly retain His equality with God, but emptied Himself, took upon Him the form of a servant, and appeared among men in the fashion of a man. This was not all. Appearing among men as one truly man, He humbled Himself still further and went obediently to His death. Nor did He die a common, ordinary death. He died the ignominious death of one accursed, the death of the lowest malefactor. He died the death of a cross, a death reserved for the outcasts of society.

But as His humiliation was the lowliest, His exaltation was the highest: "Far above all principality, and power, and might, and dominion, and every name that is named, not only in this world [age], but also in that which is to come" (Eph 1:21). He abides, living, preeminent, sovereign, with power, dignity, and majesty unsurpassed. To the name and majesty of Jesus every knee shall bow and pay homage, and every tongue shall confess that "Jesus Christ is Lord, to the glory of God the Father" (Phil 2:11).

This is the great divine pattern which was "in Christ Jesus." This picture, drawn by the hand of God, does not appear here to excite our admiration, to stir us to wonder—although it does move us to such feeling and expression—but it is here to arouse us to imitation, to embody and reflect the mind of Christ.

In the church at Philippi, rivalry and selfishness, although perhaps disguised in fairer forms, had bred difficulty and disturbance. The same hurtful forces are present in churches today and often run riot in Christian assemblies. How shall the ugliness and the hatefulness of everyday selfishness, everyday self-assertion, everyday self-interest, everyday strifes of believers be impressed upon our minds? How are we to be stirred and awakened to our true calling in humility and lowliness for the interests of others? The answer lies in the sublime words of the text: "This be minding in you, which was also in Christ Jesus." This is the will of God for us, as revealed in His Word.

Exposition

1

THE PREEXISTENCE OF CHRIST

Who, being in the form of God (Phil 2:6).

Modern theology is set against the teaching of the preexistence of the Lord Jesus Christ. Liberal theologians give no place to the doctrine and exclude from this great passage in Philippians all reference to a preexistent state. "In fact," says Fred B. Craddock, "the word *preexistence* does not fit comfortably in the vocabulary of western man. It has an exotic ring. It seems a fugitive word, escaped from a seance, wandering among us, but not at home on the well-lighted stretch of our empirical thoughts. It is not that we are unfamiliar with the word. We are—at least—with the idea."[1] Liberal theologians begin with Christ's birth at Bethlehem and make Him a mere man of ordinary birth, though with a God-consciousness not possessed by other men. However, any true view of Christ's life should give attention to that phase of His existence before He became man. It is completely unfair to sketch only His thirty-three years in the world of men, and to maintain, as they do, that the Lord's self-emptying must be limited wholly to His earthly life.

But any discussion as to whether the Lord's self-emptying refers to the preexistent Christ or to the historical person seems totally irrelevant to Paul's thought. As Kennedy says,

1. Fred B. Craddock, *The Pre-existence of Christ in the New Testament*, p. 11.

"For him his Lord's career was one and undivided. To suggest that he did not conceive a preexistence in heaven is to ignore the very foundations of his thinking."[2]

Modernist theological writers go on to state that the title "Christ Jesus," which is assigned to the Lord in this passage, is not appropriate as a designation of the Son prior to His incarnation. But as Dr. McClain has pointed out,

> This objection has little weight. Even common usage is against it; no one thinks it inaccurate, for instance, to speak of the "childhood" of President Coolidge, though, strictly speaking, *President* Coolidge had no childhood. And the objection fails utterly when we find the Apostle Paul applying the historical name to the Son of God in other passages where the reference to His pre-existent state is unmistakable (cf. Heb. 11:26, and 1 Cor. 10:4, "The Rock was Christ").[3]

The very fact of Christ's unsurpassed exemplary conduct argues strongly for His preexistence. The eternal Son of God condescending to come down into the earthly realm to save men from their sins is the supreme example to set before Christians whose natural disposition is selfishness. If someone objects that such an example as this is not within the capability of mere human beings to imitate, he does not understand the real sense of this great passage. The appeal is not for some mechanical reaction and a resultant artificial imitation of the Lord's great act of self-emptying. Rather, the Holy Spirit is constraining us to have the same mind that was in Christ—that mind which impelled Him to humble Himself to servanthood and to die on a cross in the interest of others.

The exclusion of the fact of preexistence from the passage

---

2. H. A. A. Kennedy, "Epistle to the Philippians," in *Expositor's Greek Testament*, 3:435.
3. Alva J. McClain, "The Doctrine of the Kenosis in Philippians 2:5-8," *Biblical Review* 13 (October 1928):512.

makes the words impossible to understand. The reality of Christ's preexistence must be admitted into the reckoning of the Christian mind. There must be no doubt of its genuineness despite the fact that it may not be fully understood. Anyone who seriously considers the person of Jesus Christ must also seriously consider the New Testament evidence of the Lord's preexistence. Dr. McClain has written:

> The early Church was familiar with this idea, and a reference to it in connection with the act of incarnation would need no explanation. It was part of the common faith. But if we eliminate this idea, and make the self-emptying something that took place entirely within the earthly life of Christ, at once the plea of the Apostle becomes vague and unintelligible. To what particular act in His earthly life could the language of vv. 6-7 be applied with any measure of certainty beyond mere guess-work? And why is there no hint or clue to guide the reader in fixing upon it? True, His whole life was characterized by a constant and gracious self-forgetfulness, but the aorist tense of the verb ("emptied") favors a definite act, once for all, and not simply a habit of living. The conclusion is compelling: the Apostle speaks of the one act which needed no explanation to the Philippians, that sublime and voluntary act of incarnation wherein the Word "became flesh and tabernacled among us" in servant form. The high background of this act is set forth in the phrase "existing in the form of God," a phrase which not only refers to a pre-existent state, but also has somewhat to say regarding its character.[4]

The words "who, being in God's form" offer two aspects of the Lord's preexistence: (1) the fact of His preexistence, and (2) the form of His preexistence. We shall consider them in that order.

THE FACT OF CHRIST'S PREEXISTENCE

The simple pronoun "who" (Gr., *hos*), the first word of

4. Ibid., pp. 506-7.

verse 6, will not escape the notice of the careful reader. It occupies a key position, standing like a bridge connecting two great continents, and is vitally important, for it is the link between verse 5 and the rest of the paragraph. It points back to the person of Jesus Christ, and forward to something mighty and unsurpassed about Him. He is the One of whom the following awesome facts are stated, and the One who is supreme in those facts. So with "who," the apostle Paul fixes our attention upon Christ, the One who is at the crest of glory but who for our sakes trod the paths of men. As Lenski remarks, "We must get the dramatic demonstrative effect."[5] An apt rendering of the clause might be: "That very One who was in the form of God."

To suggest that Paul did not teach the preexistence of Christ is to deny the very foundation of his doctrine. Yet the most elaborate theories have been reared by many theologians and churchmen on this passage. Their aim is to get a Christ emptied of some or all of His attributes of deity. Their whole purpose is to show that Christ is not God, that He was not preexistent. But either all this passage says of Christ is true, or it is not. All that "who" stands for is true, or it is not. Lenski is correct when he says, "This is no mere squabble of theologians."[6] It involves the whole doctrinal concept of God, His person, and His plan. It involves the entire redemptive purpose and work of the Lord Jesus Christ. The great vital issue is the Christian faith itself, and it is not an overstatement to say that the whole of the Christian faith depends upon it. Therefore, this issue must concern every true Christian believer, it is one that involves the whole church. Either we believe that Christ is sovereign Deity and that He was thus preexistent in the form of God, or we do not believe it.

Many churches in our day have left this great truth, and

5. R. C. H. Lenski, *The Interpretation of St. Paul's Epistles to the Galatians, to the Ephesians, and to the Philippians*, p. 776.
6. Ibid., p. 778.

having departed from it, have assumed a stance against it. Some are indifferent toward the matter, content to let men think as they will. Others have joined forces with anti-Christian groups that campaign actively for a human-only Jesus. This departure from the truth involves both leaders and those who are led. The current Christological disarray in Christendom is reminiscent of Jeremiah 5:31, "The prophets prophesy falsely, and the priests bear rule by their means; and my people love to have it so." Second Timothy 4:3 states: "For the time will come when they will not endure sound doctrine; but after their own lusts, shall they heap to themselves teachers having itching ears; and they shall turn away their ears from the truth, and shall be turned unto fables." In these times of rapidly mounting apostasy and spiritual dereliction, the people who make up the local church assemblies need to have a correct Christology, and they must know its meaning and importance.

But although so much is involved, the fact remains that against all who attack and deny the Person of this passage is arrayed the whole body of the Holy Scriptures, the complete testimony of the Word of God. The indispensable pronoun "who" stands at the threshold of verse 6, a shining light, triumphantly illuminating the way through this mighty passage. It reveals to us that the subject of all that follows in verses 6-11 is the "Christ Jesus" of verse 5, set forth in verse 6 in His preexistent state, with His incarnate form introduced in verse 7. In a most remarkable way, Paul connects to "who" the entire compendium of the history of Jesus Christ! With it, the apostle links the Lord's prehuman state to His entire earthly conduct. He shows Christ to be true God and true man; while He was man, He never ceased to be God. So in dealing with the evil energy of selfishness and pride, and to repudiate the speculative questions and false views of Christ, Paul, under inspiration, turns directly to the central truth of Christianity: the person of Jesus Christ. Here he finds the type set, the objective standard fixed, of what Christianity is and what it means. In bringing this out, the apostle makes a truly remarkable statement concerning the incarnation and the history of our Lord Jesus Christ. At the same time he reveals the importance he himself places on the fact of Christ coming into the world of men. He bids us to recognize in Christ the supreme example of One who looked away from His own things with infinite concern for the things of others. This is so deeply at the root of the Lord's redemptive work to save us from our sins that the principle becomes imperative and supreme for all true believers. The statement of Bishop Moule is fitting here:

> What a comment this is upon the fallacy of religious thought, which would dismiss Christian doctrine to the region of theorists and dreamers in favor of Christian life. Christian doctrine, rightly so-called, is simply the articulate statement according to the Scriptures of eternal truths and vital facts, that we may live by them. The passage before us is charged to the brim with doctrine of the person and natures of Christ.[7]

In this classic passage we find a chain of mysterious and marvelous assertions about Christ, not in the least in the manner of controversy but in the tone of a settled, living certainty. These great assertions on the one hand assure us that Jesus Christ is man in nature, in circumstances, in experience, and particularly in His relation to God the Father. But they also assure us, in exactly the same manner and tone, that He is as genuinely divine as He is genuinely human. Moreover, this passage testifies that prior to His becoming man, He was in the "form of God." In verse 7 He is described as "emptying Himself" and assuming the likeness of men. His "being in the form of God" (v. 6) is as important and essential to our faith and state as believers as His being "made in the likeness of men" (v. 7).

7. H. C. G. Moule, *Philippian Studies,* p. 103.

The verb rendered "being" in verse 6 is the first stone in the great doctrinal arch in this passage. Its importance and significance are impressed upon us by the Holy Spirit's use of the word to set forth *the fact* of Christ's preexistence. Careful attention must be given to its meaning.

The verbal expression chosen by the Holy Spirit for use in this statement by Paul is not the usual word to designate "being."[8] It is the verb *huparchōn,* which appears in the writings of the early Greek scholars to express variously: "begin, begin doing, do first, begin to be." The New Testament writers, directed by the Holy Spirit, adopted this word and used it in the general sense of "prior existence, extant," denoting an original condition extended into the present. It is used with this meaning fifty-nine times in the New Testament Scriptures.

Matthew first used the word in his record of the Lord's address to the wealthy young ruler: "If thou wilt be perfect, go and sell that thou hast" (Matt 19:21). The words "that thou hast" are a rendering of the verb *huparchō* and describe the ruler's possessions. While the word here sets forth the present reality of the young man's possessions, at the same time it signifies prior existence. For the property and assets of the ruler must be referred to the past, both as to their origin and the young man's coming into possession of them. Clearly, it describes the ruler's worldly belongings and riches, which he began to accumulate in the past, and was still gathering at the time of his confrontation with Christ.

Paul used the word to designate Peter's ancestry: "If thou, being a Jew" (Gal 2:14). It is quite obvious that at the time of the controversy at Antioch, Peter was racially exactly what he had been all his life. Originally, basically, presently, Peter was a Jew.

8. Two other words are more generally used: *eimi,* "being," and *ginomai,* "coming to pass." See these two verbs contrasted in John 8:58, by the declaration of our Lord Jesus Christ: "Before Abraham *was* [genesthai], I *am* [eimi]" (italics added).

Paul used this word again in Philippians 3:20, to describe the fact that "our citizenship is in heaven." The significance here is plain. The great commonwealth in which the saved are citizens has its fixed location in heaven, where its Head abides. Its existence does not date back from the moment of the first conversion, or from the entrance of the first citizen into it. Rather, it is fixed by divine decree and prepared by God for the redeemed. It is *now* what and where it has been from the beginning in the eternal, sovereign plan of God.

We must carry on a little further in order to appreciate the full weight of this verb. The root of the word is *archō*, to which the preposition *hupo* has been prefixed. *Archō* is a verb of origin, signifying the "first form of something, the first stage of existence of something." It is based on the word *archē*, which signifies "beginning, original, primeval, first cause." It is the word used in John 1:1 to designate the *beginning*. In composition, the preposition *hupo* expresses "place, position under," with the sense of "basic reality, that which is foundational and fundamental, actual existence upon a firm base." Thus, from the standpoint of usage and structure, this unique verb *huparchō* speaks with weight. It testifies to original existence and describes a state of being, or continuing to be, in the beginning. It has a backward look into a fundamental original condition which is protracted into the present.

With reference to Christ, the word denotes the fact that our Lord had a previous existence that consisted in a state of being in the beginning and from the beginning. While the verb does not positively assert eternal existence, it does denote prior existence, and is entirely congruous with the pre-incarnate being of the Lord Jesus Christ.[9] Appropriately,

9. Bishop Lightfoot comments on the verb *huparchō*: "The word denotes prior existence, but not necessarily eternal existence. The latter idea however follows in the present instance from the conception of the divinity of Christ which the context supposes" (*Saint Paul's Epistle to the Philippians*, p. 110).

then, the verb *huparchō* ("being") points to the original condition of Christ, His state of existence prior to the act of incarnation described in verse 7, thus establishing the fact of His preexistence. It shows clearly that the time when our Lord gave expression to His essential nature of deity was prior to His becoming incarnate in human flesh as the man Christ Jesus.

Hence, Christ is to be recognized as already existing before the beginning of His earthly history. For the apostle Paul, it was a fixed thing, a blessed fact, that the One who was born in Bethlehem of Judea preexisted in a glorious nature, and took our nature by a notable, unsurpassed condescension. His preexistence is the first thing to consider when we would attempt to understand how Christ, being true man, differs from other men. If He is God, then we must believe in His preexistence, even if the Scriptures were to say nothing about it. However, the biblical evidence for the preexistence and deity of Christ is ample. It does not rest merely upon a few scattered proof texts but is woven into the very texture of the entire New Testament. In fact, the New Testament writers almost exhaust the resources of human language in order to describe the entrance into human life of Him who, as God, had always existed and therefore is different from other men. In particular, John, Paul, and the writer to the Hebrews all testify to the preexistence of Christ in a most expressive and emphatic way.

THE TESTIMONY OF JOHN

Since the very beginning of the church, Christian believers have never doubted the significance of the introductory words of the gospel of John, "In the beginning was the Word, and the Word was with God, and the Word was God. The same was in the beginning with God." Even the first readers of John's gospel must have observed the similarity between the opening words of John 1:1 and the first words of Genesis 1:1. Both passages point to the beginning. The beginning in Genesis 1:1 points to the original creation and comes down through the course of time. In John 1:1, the beginning faces about and looks back into eternity before time was, but there finds the Word (*ho logos*). There is no doubt as to the identity of this Word. The testimony of true Christian leaders from the first century to the twentieth is unanimous: the Word is Jesus Christ. In the word *logos* is contained all that Christ was in His preexistence, all that He became in human form, and all that He is in Himself.[10]

Perhaps someone might still ask, When did the Word begin? John 1:1-2 gives a masterful answer to this question. The first clause, "In the beginning was the Word" declares that the Word preceded the creation of all things. In the beginning the Word already was. Four times in these two verses, the verb "was" lays stress upon the continuing state of the Word, that is, the Word's eternal existence. The Word was before all things because His existence had no beginning. The Word existed before anything else began. But that is not to say that the Word Himself had a beginning in the common sense. The Word belonged to the order of eternity. As Lange says,

> The Logos was not merely existent however in the beginning, but was *the efficient principle*, the beginning of the beginning. . . . And when it is said the Logos was in the beginning, His eternal existence is already expressed, and His eternal position already indicated thereby.[11]

10. "The Word" (*ho logos*) is the title given to the Lord Jesus Christ by the apostle John. He is "The Word was made [became] flesh" in John 1:14, and "The Word of God" of Revelation 19:13. He is the absolute "Yea" in all the promises of God, specifically in 2 Corinthians 1:19-20, to whom the true church answers in unison "Amen!" He is Himself the Amen (Rev 3:14).

11. Edward D. Yeomans, *The Gospel of John,* in Lange's *Commentary on the Holy Scriptures,* 17:54.

Another strong testimony to the Lord's preexistence is found in John 6. In verses 38 and 41, Christ declares that He came down from heaven. The Jews objected to this statement and murmured against Him, for they understood Him to refer to a literal descent from a literal heaven. Can a man descend from the abode of God? The Jews knew His earthly parents, so they asked, "Is not this Jesus, the son of Joseph, whose father and mother we know?" Then they added, "How is it then that he saith, I came down from heaven?" (v. 42).

If they had misunderstood the Lord, if He did not mean to teach that He had previously existed, that He had lived in heaven before He came to earth, then He should properly have corrected their misunderstanding by explaining what He did mean. Surely He was under obligation to do this, in view of the fact that His words plainly stated that He had lived in heaven before coming to earth. But the Lord did not correct them. He did not infer that they had misunderstood Him. He did not change His declaration. He forbade them to murmur at His words (v. 43). He expostulated with them and suggested that if they were offended at His words, what would they say if they were to see Him ascend to the same heaven where He was before? (v. 62).

Note the presence of the imperfect verb "was" (*ēn*) in verse 62, indicating the fact of Christ's preexistence. If these words mean anything at all, they mean that Christ lived in heaven before He came down to earth, and they correspond to the idea in the verb *huparchōn*. Moreover, they are a definite rebuke to unbelief. The implication is plain indeed: unbelief cannot stand in the light of who and what Jesus Christ really is. As Lenski states:

> The implication is the same as it was in the entire discourse:
> How can unbelief find justifiable room when men are shown
> who Jesus is? When you shall see the Son of Man ascending

up where He was before—? What then? How then can you maintain your unbelief?[12]

John brings forward another strong testimony to the Lord's preexistence in his record of Christ's words to the Jewish leaders. Jesus said, "Verily, verily, I say unto you, Before Abraham was, I am" (John 8:58). Previously Jesus had said, "Your father Abraham rejoiced to see my day: and he saw it, and was glad" (v. 56); the Jews understood Him to mean that He and Abraham had seen each other, for they replied: "Thou art not yet fifty years old, and hast thou seen Abraham?" (v. 57). The Lord did not intimate that they misunderstood Him; on the contrary, He, much to their astonishment, laid claim to an existence before Abraham was: "Before Abraham *was, I am*" (italics added).

The significance of "was" (*genesthai*) and "I am (*egō eimi*) is important and instructive. The distinction between the two should be carefully marked. Christians must understand the importance of this item of Greek grammar because it is vital to their correct knowledge of the person of Christ. The first verb, used to describe the existence of Abraham, connotes an existence that has an origin. It could be rendered "was born." Or it might be translated "came to be, entered the realm of human life." But the verb which Christ applies to Himself (*eimi*), along with the emphatic personal pronoun (*egō*), speaks of an existence that has no origin. There is no implied beginning in the verb *eimi*. It is the signature of the eternal God who identified Himself to Moses as the "I AM" (Exod 3:14). Bishop Lightfoot remarks: "The *becoming* only can be rightly predicated of the patriarch, the *being* is reserved for the eternal Son alone."[13] Thus, in the simplest terms,

12. Lenski, *The Interpretation of St. John's Gospel*, p. 508.
13. Others, too, besides Lightfoot, such as Alford, Hovey, Vincent, and Lenski, call special attention to this point as clearly established by the two verbs, "was" and "I am."

Christ testified to the eternal, divine preexistence of His person.

A further outstanding passage in John that testifies to the Lord's preexistence is chapter 17. John 17 is fitly called "The Lord's Prayer," for in it Christ prays for Himself, for the apostles, and for all believers. Verses 5 and 24 of this high-priestly prayer speak directly to Christ's preexistence and need little comment. There is no figurative or parabolic language here. On the contrary, it is remarkable for its severe simplicity of style. A sequence of points may be observed, which speak clearly in their own right:

1. The Lord prays that the Father will glorify Him (v. 5).
2. He asks for the glory which He had previously possessed in union with the Father (v. 5).
3. He was in possession of this glory "before the world was" (v. 5).
4. He adds the statement that the Father loved Him before the world's foundation (v. 24).

Thus in the simplest, clearest language possible, Christ Himself set forth the fact of His preexistence. He spoke of His preexistence with the Father and His possession of divine glory as a matter of personal consciousness. Here again is the very idea corresponding to that found in the verb *huparchōn*.

THE TESTIMONY OF PAUL

Two notable passages from Paul's other epistles help to undergird the doctrine of Christ's preexistence so eloquently set forth in his epistle to the Philippians. The first is 2 Corinthians 8:9, "For ye know the grace of our Lord Jesus Christ, that, though he was rich, yet for your sakes he became poor, that ye through his poverty might be rich."

Many people who live through both wealth and poverty find the reverse to be true; they begin with a little and gradually accumulate more. Those who begin with a great deal of wealth yet die destitute are called spendthrifts or wastrels, and we consider them unfortunate.

Christ fits the second pattern, but with infinitely different causes and consequences. Second Corinthians 8:9 tells us that the Lord was rich and then became poor. But did He ever possess a chest of worldly treasures? No, His earthly life was in the style of the lower middle class. He never lacked the essentials, but He never accumulated financial capital and worldly possessions. Since our Lord's earthly life was modest, His life of riches must predate His human birth. His being rich must describe a state prior to His earthly life. In short, it was a preexistent life.

The Unitarian-modernist contention that the verb "became poor" (*eptocheusen*) does not mean "became poor" but rather "be poor" is erroneous. The text would then mean that Christ was in reality rich but actually lived in poverty. Classical Greek allows the meaning "be poor," but the biblical use of the verb is not precisely the same. The word occurs only once in the New Testament, but appears five times in the Septuagint, and in each case it means "became poor."[14] The use of the verb in these five passages is sufficient to show the incorrectness of the Unitarian-modernist interpretation. Barnes comments:

> The riches of the Redeemer here referred to stand opposed to that poverty which He assumed and manifested when He dwelt among men. It implies: (1) His preexistence, for He became poor. He had been rich, yet not in this world. He did not lay aside wealth in this world after He had possessed it, for He had none. He was not first rich, and then poor on earth, for He had no earthly wealth. The Socinian interpreta-

14. See Judges 6:6; 14:15; Psalm 34:10; 79:8; Proverbs 23:21.

tion is, that He was rich in power and in the Holy Ghost; but it was not true that He laid these aside and that He became poor in respect to either of them. He had power even in His poverty, to still the waves, and to raise the dead, and He was always full of the Holy Spirit. But He was poor, His family was poor, His parents were poor, and He Himself was poor all His life. This then, must refer to a state of antecedent riches before His assumption of human nature.[15]

The second Pauline passage is Colossians 1:17, "And he is before all things, and by him all things consist." A simple reading of the verse leads to the conclusion that it undoubtedly refers to the preexistence of Christ. The preposition "before" (*pro*) denotes that which is prior in time to all other things.[16] Although superiority, sovereignty, and exaltation are implied in the context, it is the idea of *priority* that is emphasized. The One through whom everything was called into existence necessarily existed before all else was created. Prior to this creative work, Christ filled all the unmeasured periods of an unbeginning eternity. He preexisted all matter and material things. Everything is posterior to Him. All created things celebrate a point of origin. Christ does not, in terms of His divine existence. Notice also that the present tense is employed in the first clause of verse 17—"And he *is* before all things," not He "*was*." This further emphasizes that at every point of His existence it may be said of Him that "He *is*."[17]

---

15. Albert Barnes, *Notes on the Second Epistle to the Corinthians,* p. 519.
16. See Luke 21:12, "But *before* all these" (italics added).
17. The Greek has the emphatic pronoun *autos* ("He Himself") in verse 17. Unless this pronoun is added for emphasis, there is no satisfactory explanation for its presence in the sentence. It has been suggested by Lightfoot that *autos estin* ("He Himself is") corresponds exactly with *egō eimi* ("I Myself am") in John 8:58. Whatever may be held with regard to this point, the fact remains that "firstborn" (Col 1:15), the differentiation between Christ and the creation (v. 16), the "before all things" (v. 17*a*), and the "by him all things consist" (v. 17*b*) all point out with great clarity the preexistence of our Lord Jesus Christ.

THE TESTIMONY OF HEBREWS

The great passage of Hebrews 1:1-3 is a crowning testimony to the person of the Son of God. Having set forth the fact of God's speaking in the prophets during the extended period of the Old Testament, the writer then testifies to God's more recent speaking in His Son. The Old Testament is no less than God speaking. He has now spoken in the person of the Son through the entire New Testament. Beyond this there is no further revelation of the eternal God; nothing further will God ever speak to man. Those who constantly seek new revelations from God will never find them. These verses are God's answer to them.

Verse 2 tells of the person of the Son and of His transcendent glory, describing how the Son unites in Himself the whole of God's revelation. The Son is the great channel through whom all creation was wrought. In the very beginning God made the ages through the Son, with a view to the Son's being the Heir and, in the fullness of time, having the whole vast inheritance as the God-man.

The clause "by whom also he made the ages" reaches back to the Son's preexistence, to His preincarnate state. The equation is not difficult. If God created all things through the Son, then the Son must have existed with God the Father prior to the creating work. From all eternity, before the founding of the ages and all that exists in them, the Son was named Heir of all things and the Agent of creation. He is Heir not according to His sovereign deity, which can inherit nothing, but according to His true humanity, which inherits "all things." Then the Son, in His sovereign, eternal glory, came down to earth in the incarnation to complete the great saving work and thereafter to return to glory (v. 3).

Hebrews 1:10 is then brought in to reiterate the fact of the Son's preexistent state: "Thou, Lord, in the beginning hast laid the foundation of the earth; and the heavens are the works of thine hands." The incarnate Son is also the pre-existent Creator. In the beginning He laid the earth's foundation. This expression takes us back to the fathomless, incalculable ages of ages. Yet the preexistence of the Son takes us back even beyond that, to the incomprehensibly remote eternities of eternity. Just as the artist existed before the portrait that he painted, and the architect before the building that he designed, so God the Son existed before the universe that He brought into being. Our limited minds cannot grasp all this; the hugeness of it is beyond us. We can proceed as far as the Holy Scriptures go, but we cannot, dare not, go any further. The One who is the eternal, preincarnate Word of God, the Son preexistent, is the One by whom the heaven and the earth were made. And even though they may perish, He remains unchangeable and eternal; His abiding and eternality guarantee the permanent abiding of His people.

The evidence of Christ's preexistence stands with indisputable strength and certainty. Even Dr. Noah Worcester, a prominent Unitarian, once said, "It is amazing that the preexistence of Christ should be denied by any man who professes a respect for the oracles of God."[18] We do not in any sense endorse the Unitarian view of our Lord's natures and person, yet Dr. Worcester's statement regarding belief in Christ's preexistence is indeed interesting, surprising, and worthy of note. He maintains that, if one believes in the truthfulness of Scripture, he cannot escape believing in Christ's preexistence.

The testimony of John the Baptist to Christ's preexistence is particularly stressed by the apostle John in his gospel. Twice the apostle records the testimony of John the Baptist to the Lord's preexistence: "This was he of whom I spake, He that cometh after me is preferred before me: for he was before me" (John 1:15; cf. John 1:30). These words cannot possibly refer to the physical birth of the Lord, for John was born

18. As quoted by Richard N. Davies, *The Doctrine of the Trinity*, p. 40.

six months before Christ. The preexistence of which John the Baptist spoke with such emphasis corroborates the statements of the apostle John that the Word became flesh, and that He possessed the glory of the only begotten of the Father. John the Baptist's striking testimony embodied what the prophets spoke and wrote, for they bore witness of the same blessed, eternal Person, "whose goings forth have been from of old, from everlasting" (Mic 5:2). The words of the forerunner speak of the eternal Son of God, who became flesh, dwelt among men, and manifested God's glory. They point to the One who *was* in all eternity, and who *was* in unchanging, timeless existence.

If the Lord Jesus Christ existed before He was born in Bethlehem, the question immediately arises, Do the Old Testament Scriptures reveal to us anything about His preexistence? Does He appear anywhere in the Old Testament in His preexistent state? Is it reasonable to assume that if He did preexist, He should appear in the Old Testament era? Does it really matter whether He may be found in the Old Testament? Is there any value in this for us today?

We may unhesitatingly answer "yes" to all of these questions. Our Lord Jesus Christ does appear in the Old Testament, not merely in the Messianic prophecies but in person, and this is of the greatest significance and value in our day. His appearances may be divided into two modes.

First, He appears as the "angel of the LORD." There are many passages where this Angel is found, so there is no lack of proof texts. For example, in Genesis 16:7, 10, 11, the Angel of the LORD appears to Hagar in the desert. The Angel is called both "LORD" and "God" in verse 13, and such powers are attributed to Him as belong only to God. In Genesis 22 is the narrative of Abraham's offering of Isaac and the interposition of the Angel of the LORD. In verses 11 and 15, the title appears in the Angel's address to Abraham. The Angel calls Himself "God" in verse 12: "for now I know that thou fearest *God,* seeing thou hast not withheld thy son, thine only son, from *me*" (italics added).

Another striking example is found in Genesis 48:15-16. When Jacob blessed the sons of Joseph, he said, "The Angel [The Angel of the LORD] which redeemed me from all evil, bless the lads." The expressions "the God" in verse 15, and "the Angel" in verse 16, belong together: "The God. . . . The Angel." Jacob offered this Angel worship and attributed his redemption from evil to Him. It is impossible and inconceivable that the Angel here identified as God could be a created angel.

In the notable Scripture Exodus 3:1-18, the Angel of the LORD reveals Himself to Moses at the burning bush. A comparison of verses 2, 4, 6, 13, and 14 sweeps aside all doubt as to the identity of the Angel. The Angel of the LORD in verse 2 is the Lord and God of verse 4, and the God of Abraham, Isaac, and Jacob of verse 6. In verses 13 and 14, His name is identified as "I AM THAT I AM." The Angel of the LORD at the burning bush not only exercises governing authority but demands and receives from Moses the homage belonging to supreme Deity. Again the Angel of the LORD appears to Samson's mother, to announce her bearing a son, and is present to speak with the father of Samson, according to Judges 13:3-23.

The Angel described in these passages can be identified as the Lord Jesus Christ in His preexistent state. When Manoah, whose wife would soon give birth to Samson, asked the Angel, "What is thy name?" (Judg 13:17), the Angel replied, "Wherefore askest thou after my name, seeing it is wonderful?" (v. 18, ASV). The Hebrew word "wonderful" in this verse is the same word that appears in the great prophecy of Isaiah 9:6, "For unto us a child is born, unto us a son is given: and the government shall be upon his shoulder: and his name shall be called Wonderful [Heb., *pehleh*]." This positively identifies the Angel with the Son, the second Person of the Godhead and the Saviour born of a virgin in human flesh to take away our sins. The same word occurs also in Isaiah 28:29, which manifests the absolute deity of the Angel. It is indeed remarkable that the Angel of the LORD never reappears after the virgin birth of Christ in Bethlehem.

Second, Christ appears in the Old Testament under the name "Jehovah." The prophecy of John the Baptist and his mission in Isaiah 40:3, reads: "The voice of him that crieth in the wilderness, Prepare ye the way of the LORD [Heb., *Jehovah*]." When Matthew quoted Isaiah, he used the Greek equivalent of the word Jehovah, which is *kurios,* a title which is commonly attributed to Christ in the New Testament. In Romans 10:9, Jesus is again identified as "Lord" (Gr., *kurios;* Heb., *Jehovah*). And this is the name given to Christ again in Philippians 2:11, "And that every tongue should confess that Jesus Christ is Lord [Gr., *kurios;* Heb., *Jehovah*] to the glory of God the Father." Peter quotes from Isaiah 8:13-14 in his first epistle, 2:7-8, and refers to the Lord Jesus Christ as "a stone of stumbling, and a rock of offence." The prophecy of Isaiah 8:13-14 identifies Christ as "The LORD [Heb., *Jehovah*] of hosts." It is interesting that in Exodus 6:2-3, God refers to Himself with the words "I am the LORD [*Jehovah*]: and I appeared unto Abraham, unto Isaac, and unto Jacob, by the name of God Almighty, but by my name JEHOVAH was I not known to them." The Septuagint uses the Greek word *kurios* here, which is the name given to the Lord Jesus Christ in the New Testament and the word by which the Septuagint invariably renders the title *Jehovah.*

But how is it possible for the preexistent Christ to appear as both Jehovah, and the Angel of Jehovah? Is it possible for a general also to be a sergeant, or for a journeyman also to be an apprentice? The analogy throws us off target, for indeed, while a general wears three stars and a sergeant three chevrons, and never are the two confused, it is indeed fitting that Jesus Christ should be called by His divine title and also by a title that, at first reading, seems to refer to one of God's agents. The logical answer to this lies in the doctrine of the Trinity. In the New Testament, Christ is called both God and the Son of God; in the Old Testament, He is both Jehovah and the Angel of Jehovah. He is also called the Servant of Jehovah. The names *God* and *Jehovah* may apply to the whole Godhead or to any Member of the Godhead. In His own person, Christ is both God and Jehovah; and in His relation to the Father, He is both the Son of God and the Angel of Jehovah. Remember also that some passages identify the Angel with God Himself. In Genesis 48:15-16, the same person is called God and the Angel; in Isaiah 63:9, the title appears, "The angel of his presence." Malachi 3:1 announces the coming of "the Lord . . . the messenger [angel]."

Now what is the value of the appearance of the preexistent Christ in the Old Testament Scriptures? Of what importance is it for us today, so far removed from the patriarchal times and the era of the prophets? How do we as believers in this period of time profit from this truth?

In the first place, it gives to the Old Testament Scriptures an abiding devotional value and makes them of infinitely more advantage and benefit to us, because it fills the Old Testament with the person of our blessed Lord. The Old Testament thus far surpasses the modern appraisal of it as compiled merely for the Jews, with a record of their experiences; their laws, statutes, and chronicles of their kings; and their wars with the surrounding Gentile nations. It is God's revelation to us and actually belongs to every age. We find joy, profit, comfort, strength, encouragement, and instruction in reading the Old Testament, because it meets the needs of the people of God.

And beyond that, it is actually a revelation of Jesus Christ, our Lord and Saviour. The Lord said to the Jews, "Search the scriptures; for in them ye think ye have eternal life: and they are they which testify of me" (John 5:39). When He spoke of "the scriptures," Christ was, of course, referring to the Old

Testament record. The great central, unifying theme of the Old Testament is the person and work of our Lord Jesus Christ, who is present throughout it all in type, symbol, representation, illustration, promise, and prophecy.

There is a second reason the appearance of the preexistent Christ in the Old Testament holds great value for us. It completes the picture of the Son of God, so that there is nothing lacking for us. Many consider Him only in His humiliation; others, in His humiliation and the exaltation that followed. But in the Old Testament, we see Him in His preincarnate glory. We see Him as the eternal God, Jehovah, the Lord of all creation and history. We see Him as Creator of the world and of man. We see Him as the Angel of Jehovah coming to give succor to a helpless woman, Hagar, with her babe in the desert. We see Him as the great Angel moving ahead of the host of Israel, and going behind them, their Protector and Provider. We see Him instructing and strengthening Elijah and then calling him up into heaven by a whirlwind. We see Him as the destroying Angel against the Assyrian army, cutting down 187,000 soldiers in a single night. We see Him encamping around all who trust in Him, and delivering them. We see Him afflicted in the afflictions of His own, redeeming them, and bearing them in His power and grace. We see Him shutting the mouths of the lions so that they can do no harm to His servant.

Hence the Old Testament testimony to the preexistence of Christ completes the picture and gives the one whole, grand, majestic portrait of our blessed Lord, so that the statement of G. Mayer is indeed fitting: "I solemnly repeat, The eternal Godhead of Christ is the foundation of the Church, of faith, of all true Christology."[19]

The Form of Christ's Preexistence

The fact of the Lord's preexistence at once gives rise to the

19. As quoted by Lenski, *The Interpretation of St. John's Gospel*, p. 34.

question: In what form did He exist before the world's foundation? The answer to this inevitable inquiry is set forth in the first clause of Philippians 2:6, "Who, being in the form of God." In His preexistent state, then, He was in God's form. As "the form of a servant" (v. 7) implies that He was a Servant, in the same manner, "the form of God" means that He was God, unless these great words are to be stripped of their power and life. The emphatic idea is that He was in the form of God before He came to be in the form of a servant.

But what was this "form of God" (*morphē theou*) in which He existed? What was His form of preexistence?

Obviously, in arriving at a satisfactory answer to the question, it is necessary to consider the significance of the word "form" (*morphē*). In its early sense, the word was used to describe all those sensible qualities which, when striking the eye, lead us to the conviction that we are actually seeing a tangible reality. It did not carry any of the secondary ideas such as gesture, dress, motion, manner of walk, or parade, but rather indicated a definiteness that characterizes something that does not change. We may take the illustration of the "form" of a tree, a house, an automobile, a lion—the "form" of any definite thing which, as such, is one only, a real object, and involves no pretext or change.

Look at a tree. What do you see? Something green, something brown, something round or pear-shaped on top, and something long and thin that connects the green foliage to the ground. When all that information strikes our brains, we think "tree." But not all trees are the same. Some have flowers that blossom, some have leaves that are long and slender, some bear fruit, and so forth. Nevertheless, whenever we see one of these things, we think "tree." Greek philosophers explained it: Amid all the changing varieties of things we call trees, there is a form, an unchanging reality of "treeness" that we recognize in its material, and therefore changeable, manifestation as a tree. Behind the appearance is the reality. The appearance changes constantly; leaves fall off, fruit drops, buds open. But the form never changes. "Treeness" remains the same from moment to moment, day to day, year to year.

The philosophers went one step further. They claimed that because the form never changes, it alone is real. The appearances (green, vertical posture, blossoms, fruit) that we attribute to the form are merely the accidentals, the peripheral qualities, and are therefore not real. Now we may see why *morphē* is such an important word. It refers to the very essence of a thing, the unchangeable reality that expresses the identity of something, no matter how many different manifestations that thing may undergo.

We can employ the example of "treeness" only so far in our understanding of *morphē*. We never see "treeness"; we see trees. *Morphē* in the New Testament must not be taken as some kind of ethereal idea; emphasis falls rather on the constancy, the unchanging nature (theologians call it immutability) of the thing described.

Moreover, it is to be distinguished from the words "likeness, fashion, similarity," which are designated by other Greek terms in the New Testament.[20] It is an expression that describes the being of a person by adverting to the attributes with which, as it were, he is clothed. It marks out in particular those essential attributes that are characteristic of the person described, by which that person is permanently distinguished because they rise out of his nature.

For example, we are able to learn a great deal about a be-

20. "Form" (*morphē*) denotes more than "outward appearance" (*eidos*), that which strikes the eye, the shape of something, but which *may* be merely outlined or imaginary, created by the mind and eye and not really there. Luke 3:22 and 9:29 are exceptions to this, denoting in each case real appearance. The word "fashion" (*schēma*) comprises all that appeals to the senses and is fleeting, unsubstantial, changeable. Hence, Paul speaks of the "fashion" of this world age, which is changing and passing away. "Similarity" is rendered by the word *homoios,* pointing out resemblance, likeness in form or look, in appearance, in nature, and in mode of thinking, feeling, and acting. See on these terms Matthew 11:16; John 5:37; 9:9; Romans 12:2; 1 Corinthians 7:31; 2 Corinthians 5:7; 11:13-15; Revelation 1:13, 15.

liever's inner self and true spiritual condition by his outward bearing and expression. A genuinely saved man will show outwardly his inward state by the things he says and does, by his actions and general behavior. If his spiritual condition is wrong, it is certain that there will be expressions of it. His spiritual delinquency will be seen despite attempts to conceal it.

The word "form" (*morphē*) appears but three times in the New Testament Scriptures, twice in this passage, and in Mark 16:12. It is used to denote that particular expression of being which carries in itself the distinctive nature and character of that being to whom it pertains. Therefore, it is permanently identified with that nature and character. Vincent says of *morphē:*

> As applied here to God, the word is intended to describe that mode in which the essential being of God expresses itself. We have no word which can convey this meaning, nor is it possible for us to formulate the reality. *Form* inevitably carries with it to us the idea of *shape*. It is conceivable that the essential personality of God may express itself in a mode apprehensible by the perception of pure spiritual intelligence; but the mode itself is neither apprehensible nor conceivable by human minds. This mode of expression, this "setting" of the divine . . . essence . . . is the perfect expression of a perfect essence. It is not something imposed from without, but something which proceeds from the very depth of the perfect being, and into which that being perfectly unfolds, as light from fire.[21]

Thus it may be said that "form of God" (*morphē theou*) refers to the external, real expression of the internal nature and character of the eternal God. McClain's extended comment must be added here:

---

21. Marvin R. Vincent, *The Epistle to the Philippians*, in *Word Studies in the New Testament*, 3:431.

The general meaning of *form* is external appearance, that form by which a person or thing strikes the vision. Our English word "form" scarcely expresses its full significance. Quite often we use this term to indicate the very opposite of reality, saying of something that it is only a *form*, by which we mean that the external appearance of the thing is misleading and does not truly represent the inner substance or character. Thus, some have argued, Christ was a *form* of God; He was God-like, but not God. The word "form" seems to strike deeper than this. Lightfoot, Trench, Bengel, and others, argue convincingly against a number of those who think otherwise, that *form* is something intrinsic and essential as opposed to *fashion*, which is merely outward and more or less accidental. Following this idea, S. G. Green, in his Handbook to the Grammar of the Greek Testament, defines "form" (*morphe*) as the form which is "indicative of the interior nature." It is indeed external form, that which strikes the eye, but as such it accurately represents the underlying nature from which it springs. If this be the significance of the term, then to say that Christ Jesus was "existing in the form of God" is to affirm that He was very God manifesting Himself in some external form through which He could be known, probably to the inhabitants of heaven for what He truly was.[22]

The noun *form* appears here without the definite article, and therefore refers to the divine character and essence. Christ's outward expression of His inmost being was, in its nature, the expression of deity. The form Christ had was identical with God's form. Wuest says:

Since that outward expression which this word speaks of, comes from and is truly representative of the inward being, it follows that our Lord as to His nature is the possessor of the divine essence of deity, and being that, it also necessarily follows that our Lord is absolute deity Himself, a co-partici-

22. McClain, p. 504.

pant with God the Father and God the Holy Spirit in that divine essence which constitutes God, God.[23]

And Vincent states:

To say then, that Christ was in the form of God is to say that He existed as essentially One with God. The expression of deity through human nature (v. 7) thus has its background in the expression of deity as deity in the eternal ages of God's being. Whatever the mode of this expression, it marked the being of Christ in the eternity before creation. As the form of God was identified with the being of God, so Christ, being in the form of God, was identified with the being, nature, and personality of God.[24]

What meaning then is to be attached to "form of God" in which our Lord Jesus Christ preexisted? In what form did He exist in the ages before His appearance in human form, before the foundation of the world? Did He possess an external form which strikes the vision? Or does "form" refer to the divine attributes of God, which, in their expression, make possible the knowledge that God is God? Or is there some other explanation of His preincarnate "form"?[25]

To provide a scrupulously correct answer to these questions would require that one be allowed to peer into the very glory of the great Godhead itself. We offer a conclusion, but one

23. Kenneth S. Wuest, *Philippians in the Greek New Testament*, p. 63.
24. Vincent, p. 431.
25. It seems appropriate to remark here that most commentators are restrained in their comments on the meaning of "form of God," and rightly so. For what human mind—even renewed by the Holy Spirit—can peer into the Godhead and discern its infinite, eternal mysteries? But we have the words of the Holy Scriptures, and we shall do well to hold to *them* for our knowledge of the "form of God," and refrain from human speculation upon what is perhaps the most conspicuous and magnificent of all the inspired utterances in the New Testament. We may logically expect to receive our greatest help from the Scriptures themselves, and the surest meaning from the divinely chosen writer of the passage, the apostle Paul himself. And we should keep in mind that Paul appeals to the readers to engage in a daily life and walk of loving concern and self-forgetfulness, and as the great incentive to this end, he holds up before them the supreme example of the Lord Jesus Christ, who, on their behalf, "emptied Himself, and took upon Him the form of a slave" (Phil 2:7, author's trans.).

that must necessarily be qualified by the limitations of the natural mind, even though illuminated by the Holy Spirit. We dare not go further than God Himself has revealed. We must bow before the God of the ages and confess that it is impossible to state with inviolable accuracy the precise "form of God" in which our blessed Lord preexisted. For the manner in which the personality of God expresses itself is beyond apprehension by the finite mind, and therefore beyond description. As Robert Rainy says:

> The Apostle . . . speaks of the incarnation as that which reveals itself to us, as it offers itself to the contemplation of men. To involve himself in a discussion of inner mysteries concerning the divine nature and the human, and the manner of their union, as these are known to God, is not, and could not be his object. *The mysteries must be asserted, but much about them is to continue unexplained.*[26]

In times past God made known His presence to men by a manifestation of glory, which would create in the minds of the beholders a profound impression of majestic deity and a deep sense of reverence and awe. Exodus 24:9-10 says Moses and his companions "saw the God of Israel." What form they saw, we are not told. In Exodus 33:15, the manifestation of deity is called "thy presence." In the context following (vv. 20-23), God spoke of His "glory" but forbade Moses to see His "face." Exodus 40:34-36 calls attention to the "cloud" and says, "The glory of the LORD filled the tabernacle." In Numbers 12:8, the divine manifestation is called "the similitude of the LORD," but no explanation is given as to what that "similitude" was. In Deuteronomy 33:2, it is said that "he shined forth," yet we are not told in what form the shining forth appeared. The psalmist, referring to God's presence in Psalm 31:16, says, "thy face," and Psalm 93:1 describes God as "clothed with majesty." We are told in Isaiah 6:1-2 that the

26. Robert Rainy, "The Epistle to the Philippians," in *The Expositor's Bible,* 6:136.

prophet "*saw* . . . the Lord . . . high and lifted up" (italics added), and the passage speaks particularly of God's train that "filled the temple." Attempts to interpret and define this "train" are futile. The prophet Ezekiel, in the first chapter of his prophecy, says: "The heavens were opened, and I saw visions of God" (1:1), and the description of God's glory that follows eludes analysis by the human mind. Ezekiel concludes, "This was the appearance of the likeness of the glory of the LORD. And when I saw it, I fell upon my face" (1:28). In Daniel 7:9-10, the prophet describes "the Ancient of days . . . whose garment was white as snow, and the hair of his head like the pure wool: his throne was like the fiery flame, and his wheels as burning fire."

There is no doubt that these miraculous incidents and events are manifestations of deity and glory by which the Lord God impressed His Old Testament people with His transcendent majesty and divine nature, and prompted them to lift their hearts to Him in worship and adoration. The men who "saw" the Lord in these extraordinary instances beheld that which was real, not artificial or accidental. It may well be that the One of whom these Old Testament writers speak is the Son of God as He existed in "form of God"; that is, they saw the Son of God in that form which He possessed in His preexistent state, as He was known in that antemundane character and condition. McClain says:

> Whom and what did these men see? I am inclined to believe they saw the Son "existing in the form of God," that form which strikes the eye, and is at the same time no mere outline, or superficial resemblance, but that which is rather truly indicative of God's inner nature and invisible substance.[27]

Attempts have been made to explain these visions and displays of preexistence and deity and the terms used to describe

27. McClain, p. 505.

them, but in doing so, ideas borrowed from material sub-
stances have been generally applied to the incomprehensible
nature of spiritual being. The terms found in the Holy Scriptures such as "hand," "feet," "right arm," and "eyes" are an-
thropomorphisms employed by the writers of the sacred Word
to inculcate the minds of men with the reality of God, His
person, His presence, and His work. These terms are figures
of speech, not descriptive of God's anatomy. When God is
spoken of as appearing to the patriarchs and walking with
them, such passages are to be explained as referring to God's
temporary manifestations of Himself in human form, manifestations which prefigured the final tabernacling of God the
Son in human flesh.

Side by side with these anthropomorphic expressions and
manifestations, however, are specific declarations which forbid us to develop any purely materialistic conceptions of God.
In Isaiah 66:1, God states through the prophet: "The heaven
is my throne, and the earth is my footstool." In John 4:24, it
is recorded that our Lord said, "God is a Spirit." The apostle
Paul, describing his vision of the Lord, wrote that "he was
caught up into paradise, and heard unspeakable words, which
it is not lawful for a man to utter" (2 Cor 12:4). The apostle
speaks of the words he heard as being forbidden men to utter,
but says nothing of what he *saw*. The inference is that what
he saw was equally unlawful for men to utter, and completely
indescribable. The passage in Exodus 33:18-20 declares that
man cannot see God and live, while 1 Corinthians 2:9-16
intimates that apart from the Holy Spirit of God, men cannot know God or understand His Word.

All of this means that God is not a material being, and it
forbids our conceiving Him to be a *thing*. It does not, however, forbid our conceiving God to be *personal*. Nor does it
prohibit belief in the Son's manifestation throughout His hab-
itat of glory in that form which denotes His eternal Godhead
and divine nature and being. But humans *do* rest too much

in the material and sensuous, and we must avoid all representations of God which identify the person and being of God with the helps that are employed to assist us in realizing His presence and power. "They that worship him must worship him in spirit and in truth" (John 4:24*b*). One thing is certain: the blessed, incarnate Lord Jesus Christ provides an everlasting revelation of the invisible God in bodily form and is God's supreme provision to satisfy the longings of men to see God.

Thus we conclude that "form" (*morphē*) refers to the attributes of the great Godhead, the form and glory of which are ineffable, too lofty and sacred for adequate human expression and description. In other words, the word "form" speaks here of the form in which the Son of God preexisted, manifesting those attributes, setting forth their unutterable glory, akin to the idea expressed in John 1:1, "The Word was with God, and the Word was God." That there was a literal, external manifestation of the Son of God in His preexistent state is both probable and logical since the word "form" carries us especially to those attributes of the One described by the word. The attributes are characteristic; by them that One is distinguished to the eye or mind or both, and they denote the true nature of that One because they arise out of that nature. It is the outward expression of the internal nature of Almighty God, not assumed from without but proceeding directly from within. McClain states:

> This *form of God* may include a reference to a literal external appearance, but doubtless the more important reference is to the divine attributes. For it is through the exercise or function of these that, from an external viewpoint, God appears most truly as God. In this functioning, we find in the deepest sense the *form* of God.[28]

"Form of God" therefore is the expression of the essential

28. McClain, p. 506.

personality of God, and denotes the form in which Christ the Son was manifested in His preexistent state. It was the natural and proper expression of the divine nature. It was that form in which the essential personality of God expressed itself and functioned in a mode comprehensible to spiritual intelligence. The statement that Christ was "in the form of God" means that in His preexistent state He was actually one with God. As Vincent comments: "As the *form* of God was identified with the *being* of God, so Christ, being in God's form, was identified with the being, nature, and personality of God."[29]

To Christ, therefore, with and in the Father, we have learned to ascribe all wisdom and power, all glory and blessedness, all holiness and majesty, all greatness and authority. Especially through Him the ages were made, and in Him they hold together. The fullness, the sufficiency, the essential strength of Godhead were—and are—His. The exercise and manifestation of all these were His form of being. We might thus expect that the expression of His supremacy, transcendence, and sovereignty should be written on the face of any self-manifestation to created beings.

The notion that Christ preexisted only in the form of His human soul must be rejected as mere speculation. It is completely contrary to the teaching of the Holy Scriptures. Luke 2:11 states: "For unto you is born this day in the city of David a Saviour." In Hebrews 2:14-17, the testimony is: "He also himself likewise took part of the same [flesh and blood] . . . he took on him the seed of Abraham . . . in all things it behoved him to be made like unto his brethren." It was *the Word* who became man by virgin birth and incarnation, and not a God-man who assumed a material body. If Christ had only a body in common with the rest of mankind, then He was not true man, and He is beyond human sympathies. We need One to whom we may come in trust and love, who knows

29. Vincent, p. 431.

our needs, and who can be "touched with the feeling of our infirmities" (Heb 4:15). At the same time this extraordinary notion, in ascribing the dignity and power of the work of redemption to a sublime, preexistent human soul, totally denies the deity of Christ. For the essential point in the doctrine of Christ's preexistence is the fact that He had existence as a living being *in the form of God* before His human soul began to exist.

A single item remains for consideration. The phrase "in the form of God" is placed forward in the sentence to show that special emphasis must be placed upon these words. This particular stress in the Greek sentence is most significant. It throws into bold relief the fact that the Lord Jesus Christ was in God's form. It underlines the fundamental truth that the genuine and essential *form* in which our Lord preexisted was that of God.

Hence, we are given the major premise; the first stone in the great arch is laid. This great declaration, "Who, being in the form of God" leaves us with all doubt completely obliterated from our minds. Our blessed Lord, the One in whom we have been led to place our faith and trust, *is God*. Eternally, in the ages before time, He was in the "form of God." In time, He appeared "in the likeness of men," bringing salvation to the world. Yet He did not cease to be God. Through all the changes incident to His incarnation, He remains the same, blessed Person, our Lord and our God. The rest of the facts follow in order. We cannot help but look up "where Christ sitteth" (Col 3:1) and breathe with a constraining sense of gratitude and awe, "Thanks be to the God of all grace."

2

THE DEITY OF CHRIST

Who ... thought it not robbery to be equal with God
(Phil 2:6*b*).

We are more or less a class-conscious people. Lawyers and doctors are seen more frequently in tennis clubs than bowling alleys, and union workers are seldom country club members. We each learn our place, settle into it, and seldom attempt to cross boundaries. However, given the opportunity to move up, most of us would take it eagerly. A natural desire to climb, pride in one position or another, and the desire to possess the advantages of a higher level all compel us to seek advancement. We naturally look higher.

Our Lord Jesus Christ enjoyed a status and glory surpassed by none. He occupied the form of God. Equality with God was His by sovereign right. He did not have to strive for it as men pursue status and prestige. The glory of God was His by virtue of who He was. In the light of these considerations, the incarnation and atonement take on special meaning. Christ was so truly divine that His equality with God did not appear to Him, nor was it reckoned by Him, as anything but His own. He did not count this equality as arrogantly assumed but His by right.

Notwithstanding, He dealt with it for our sakes with a most remarkable and sublime remembrance of others, far from regarding it for Himself alone, as one who had assumed it unlawfully would have done. "Who . . . thought it not robbery to be equal with God" offers two crucial considerations: (1)

the equality of Christ with God, and (2) the exercise of the Lord's mind toward that equality.

THE EQUALITY OF CHRIST WITH GOD

Christ's equality with God is set forth in the words "To be equal with God" (*to einai isa theō*). It is obvious from the form of the clause that "who, being in the form of God" (v. 6*a*) and "to be equal with God" are immediately related. "Form of God" indicates deity in the form of its expression, and the clause "to be equal with God" must be consistent with this fact. It is certain that the One who exists "in the form of God" has the state and nature of this kind of existence. Christ could not possibly exist in the form of God without possessing the nature of God. Hence, "being in the form of God" and "to be equal with God" both express the same idea: Christ's form was "the form of God," and by nature He was "equal with God." Note McClain's statement:

> The phrase *being on an equality with God* is exegetical and explanatory of the phrase *existing in the form of God*. The only question is whether these two phrases are exactly equivalent, or whether the former adds to the latter the important idea of actual historical manifestation. This second interpretation is very suggestive and is not lacking in considerations which support it, but I prefer the first as more in harmony with the entire viewpoint. . . . In the mind of the writer then, to exist "in the form of God" is to be "equal with God," whatever else may be in the latter phrase.[1]

There are two significant facts which are derived from the expression "to be equal with God."

1. EQUALITY EXPRESSED BY "EQUAL WITH GOD"

The word translated "equal" is a three-letter term in the Greek (*isa*), a neuter plural adverb denoting the fact of equality in quality or quantity. It was used many times by

1. Alva J. McClain, "The Doctrine of the Kenosis in Philippians 2:5-8," *The Biblical Review* 13 (October 1928):505.

early Greek writers to express equality in appearance, size, strength, and number, and sometimes to denote sameness of mind and an equal, reciprocal relationship. The word was used to show something as being equally divided or distributed and to designate a person having a share equal to that of another.

Its appearances in the Holy Scriptures are not so numerous. The word occurs twice in the Septuagint and eight times in the New Testament. However, its meaning and significance are clear. The two occurrences of the word in the Septuagint are in Ezekiel 40:5-6, where it means "one." In verse 5 it describes the measurement of the breadth and height of the Temple as being the same: *one* reed. In verse 6 it designates the breadth of the gate's two thresholds as being equal: *one* reed.

In the New Testament, the word occurs first in Matthew 20:12, where it has the significance of making one equal to another in the payment of wages. In Mark 14:56, 59 the term is used twice to denote agreeing testimonies. Luke 6:34 has the word signifying recompense equal in amount to that which was loaned. John 5:18 records the Jewish accusation that Christ was "making himself *equal* with God" (italics added). The word is used here in the sense of claiming for oneself the nature, position, and authority which belong to God alone. In the passage under consideration, Paul uses *isa* to express Christ's equality of state and nature with God. Finally, the word occurs in Revelation 21:16, where the length, breadth, and height of the holy city are declared to be *the same*. It is evident from this brief examination of the general use of the word, that it denotes *sameness*, that which is equal and identical, and not mere likeness.

The significance of the word in Philippians 2:6*b* is therefore unmistakable. It denotes the *absolute equality* of Christ with God, and underscores His sameness of nature and condition in contrast to mere similarity or resemblance.[2] The phrase "equal with God" adds to the idea of *form of expression of deity* ("form of God") that of *equality of nature*.[3] Thus "equal with God" expresses the God-equal existence of our Lord Jesus Christ in His prehuman state, and He has this condition of existence because He is very God from all eternity, from everlasting to everlasting (see Psalm 90:1-2).

A host of other New Testament passages attest the truth of the equality of Christ with God as set forth by this expression "equal with God" in verse 6. It is not possible to examine all the evidence, but several outstanding passages should be considered. In John 1:1, the clause "And the Word was God" is not essentially different from the sentence "to be equal with God" and the phrase "being in the form of God."[4] As is the case with the proper noun *God* in the infinitive clause "to be equal with God" in verse 6*b* and with the same noun *God* in the expression "form of God" in verse 6*a*, the noun *God* in John 1:1 occurs without the definite article. This changes the proper noun *God* into the abstract, thus denoting the *character and essence* of deity.[5] The imperfect verb "was" (*ēn*),

2. It should be noted here that the proper noun "God" stands by itself, without the definite article, and therefore stresses quality, kind, character. Thus the force of "equal with God" appears plainly as setting forth the divine quality, or kind, of essence and nature.

3. The disagreement among scholars over the use of "equal" (*isa*) as a predicate, or as an adverb, does not greatly affect the meaning of the clause "did not count it robbery to be equal with God," and does not remove the fact of Christ's deity. Both are legitimate, although, as has been previously indicated, the sense and connection, as well as the progress of thought in the passage, may be taken as favoring the adverbial sense of *isa* ("equal"), to set forth the divine mode of existence.

4. Actually the sentence in the original Greek reads literally: "And God was the Word." But the noun carrying the definite article—in this case, "*the* Word"—acts as the subject, so that the words are reversed to read: "And the Word was God." The proper noun "God" is qualitative, pointing out character, kind, essence.

5. The nonuse of the definite article gives to a noun more of a generic quality, stressing kind and character. Generic nouns describe a class or kind of things. In English, for example, the statement "man has sinned" refers to the class of all men. However, "*the* man has sinned" points to one man and perhaps one act of sin as well. No definite article precedes "God" in either John 1:1 or Philippians 2:6. Christ is thereby identified with the character and essence of God.

which denotes ongoing, incomplete action in the past, appears three times in John 1:1 and once in verse 2. It implies uncreated being as distinct from that which is created. This distinction is set forth sharply in verse 3, where all creation is designated by a different verb: "All things *were made* [*egeneto*] by him" (italics added). In verse 2, the phrase "with God" (*pros ton theon*) denotes the individuality of the Son as He faces the Father in the Godhead. John 1:1-2 sets forth three great and indisputable facts: (1) the existence of Christ over, above, and beyond time, (2) the distinct personal existence of Christ the Son equal with the Father, and (3) the nature of Christ as very God in essence.

John 5:17-18 records that the Jews sought to kill the Lord because He said that God was His Father, "making himself equal with God." He was not guilty of attempting to make Himself equal with God, for He *was equal* with God. Christ's equality is proved by His trinitarian position and relation as revealed in this passage. He said, "The Son can do nothing of himself, but what he seeth the Father do: for what things soever he doeth, these also doeth the Son likewise" (v. 19). Christ could not perform His work separated from the Father, as though He were a totally different being. Father and Son work in concert. Christ could not and did not perform His work as an independent journeyman. He bore an indissoluble link with the Father in heaven. The same truth is set forth in verse 21, which states that in the same manner in which the Father quickens the dead, the Son also "quickeneth whom he will." Christ claimed equality with God by asserting His right to equality in honor: "All men should honour the Son, even as they honour the Father" (v. 23). Further, He affirmed His self-existence, saying, "For as the Father hath life in himself; so hath he given to the Son to have life in himself" (v. 26). The same testimony appears in John 8:28: "I do nothing of myself; but as my Father hath taught me, I speak these things."

In John 10:30, our Lord testified not only to His equality but also to His unity with God the Father when He declared, "I and my Father are one." There is mystery here, the mystery of the personal distinction of Son and Father: "I—and the Father." Yet they, in the unity of nature, *are one.* This is the open declaration of our blessed Lord, and if we would seek to penetrate this great mystery, it had better be by faith.

The Jews clearly understood these words of Christ to be a claim to equality and to unity of nature, for they took up stones to stone the Lord. They gave as their reason for such an action, "Because that thou, being a man, makest thyself God" (John 10:31, 33).

A final passage, of somewhat different character, brings forward strong evidence of equality. Titus 2:13 reads: "Looking for that blessed hope, and the glorious appearing of *the great God and our Saviour Jesus Christ*" (italics added). This statement of the New Testament is to be regarded as "a direct, definite, and even studied declaration of Christ's deity."[6] That the two proper nouns, "God" and "Saviour," denote the same Person is supported by the following facts:

1. The order of words in the genitive expression "of the great God and our Saviour" is to be taken as designating *one* person, not two.[7]
2. The term "appearing" (*epiphaneian*) is applied especially to God the Son and never to God the Father. It is the appearing of Christ that is here set forth as the event to be looked for.
3. Verse 14, the next verse, is closely related and speaks of the person of verse 13 as the One who "gave himself."

Thus the equality of Christ with God stands incontestable.

6. Charles J. Ellicott, as quoted by A. H. Strong, *Systematic Theology*, p. 307.
7. The one definite article standing before the words "great God" governs both nouns, "God," and "Saviour," and indicates that Christ is both God and Saviour. The noun "Saviour" refers to the same Person as the noun "God."

We do not hesitate to assert the absolute deity of Jesus Christ, for it is abundantly proved in the Holy Scriptures. The writers of Scripture have used every conceivable form of terminology in setting forth the deity of the One who came down from heaven to take away our sins. The doctrine of Christ's deity is diffused throughout all the Scriptures, and we should never think of Him or speak of Him without remembering this. Sir Robert Anderson wrote:

> But everything depends upon the deity of Christ; and therefore, as Athanasius said long ago, in contending for that great truth, "We are contending for all." It would seem to me therefore, that even if we could find a Scripture warrant—*and I can find none*—for liberty to name the Lord of glory with the easy familiarity so common in these evil days, we should do well to forego that liberty, and to give proof by our very words, in season and out of season, that we are of the number who honor Him "even as they honor the Father." The confession of Him thus *as Lord* is the very essence of the Gospel.[8]

Because of its peculiar interest and value, I add here the significant statement of an unusual witness, John Quincy Adams, who long ago wrote: "No argument that I have ever heard can satisfy my judgment that the doctrine of the divinity of Christ is not countenanced by the New Testament."[9] This is the testimony of a Unitarian of learning and judgment. It is true that *deity* undoubtedly means more than the *divinity* used by Adams and is a term frequently employed by today's liberal theologians. Nevertheless, this statement of Adams does bear some weight. It is similar to that of Worcester (see p. 41). Adams claimed that, if one takes Scripture literally, he must believe in Christ's divinity.

8. Sir Robert Anderson, *The Lord from Heaven*, p. 95.
9. John Quincy Adams, *Diary*, 7:229, as quoted by William Shedd, *Dogmatic Theology*, 1:313.

The vigorous denials of Christ's equality with God have not shaken the faith of those who have turned to Christ, for in Him they have found the true God and eternal life (see John 17:3). The power of the great Shepherd to give His sheep eternal life and to keep them securely, to protect them and to provide for them, is due to His equality with God. If He is merely a creature, He cannot save us from our sins, and we cannot trust His words. Apart from the deity of Christ, we have no sinless Saviour; and if Christ is not God, there is no atonement for sin. Hence, if He is not God, then in deliberately encouraging men and women to worship Him and to trust Him as their Redeemer He is the greatest impostor the world has ever known. If Christ is not God, we cannot love Him as God must be loved or worship Him as God is to be worshiped. In short, if Jesus Christ was not preexistent, if then He is not God, Christianity is only a myth, we are not saved from our sins, and our faith is vain.

But the Scriptures are not mistaken, for they are *God speaking*, and they ascribe absolute deity to Christ. The Christian revelation is the heavenly manifestation of Christ the Son of God. It is not that a great and good man once walked on this earth among other men, performed miracles, taught wonderful truths, lived a holy, sinless life because He knew more about God than any other man, and then was put shamefully to death for what He believed. But the Person who lived on earth and then died on the cross to save us from our sins was the Lord of glory, who is now on the throne of Almighty God, in all the glory of God, with all power and authority in heaven and on the earth. And as Herrmann aptly puts it, "When we confess His deity, we simply give Him the right name."[10] So we bow humbly, gratefully, before Him, with hearts full of praise, adoration, and wonder, and say, as with Thomas the apostle, "My Lord and my God" (John 20:28).

10. Herrmann, as quoted by P. C. Simpson, *The Fact of Christ*, p. 131.

2. ETERNITY EXPRESSED BY "TO BE"

The expression "to be" is the translation of the Greek present infinitive with the definite article, *to einai*. The King James Version translation should be noted for its clarity, "to be equal." The present tense denotes continuous being; it does not indicate either a beginning or an ending but points to perpetual existence. When we speak of the attribute of eternity in connection with Christ, we do not mean simply that He will never cease to be. Men and angels will never cease to exist, yet they are not eternal. Our Lord Jesus Christ is eternal; He has no beginning of existence, has always been, and will always be.

It is worthy of note that the definite article *to*, which appears with the infinitive *einai* (be), performs its normal function of identifying and particularizing the word with which it is used.[11] It points back in the sentence to "being in the form of God," emphasizing the God-equal existence which manifests itself in that form. Our Lord, then, is without beginning and without ending, keeps on being, and continues to occupy that place of equality with God. The internal aspect of that equality as related to the divine nature is designated by "equal with God" (*isa theō*), and the external aspect is expressed by "form of God" (*morphē theou*).

This testimony to the eternity of Christ is augmented by the testimony of many other passages of Scripture in which the attribute of eternity is clearly applied to the Lord. Many of these passages cannot be examined here, but I shall briefly cite certain outstanding ones. Isaiah 9:6 states in part: "And his name shall be called . . . The everlasting Father." Some object that to apply these words to Christ confounds Him with the Father. But the verse clearly relates all the titles given to the child born, the son given, who is Christ. Moreover, verse 7 identifies the same person as the Messianic King,

11. Here it means: *"That very state* of continuous being which belongs only to the Son of God, our Lord Jesus Christ."

who shall establish His Kingdom upon the throne of David. In regard to the title "everlasting Father," the statement of Barnes goes straight to the point:

> The term *Father* is not applied to the Messiah here with any reference to the distinction in the divine nature: for that word is uniformly in the Scriptures applied to the first, not to the second person in the Trinity. But it is used in reference to duration as an Hebraism, involving high poetic beauty. He is not merely represented as everlasting, but He is introduced by a strong figure, as even the Father of Eternity, as if even everlasting duration owed itself to His paternity. There could not be a more emphatic declaration of strict and proper eternity.[12]

John 8:58 is a decisive declaration of our Lord's eternality from His own lips, in which the expression "I am" denotes His timeless existence. This is unquestionably the sense of the unlimited present tense of the verb "am" (*eimi*). This use of the present "I am" is in contrast to that of "was" (*genesthai*), which describes Abraham's birth in time. (This has been previously pointed out in connection with the Lord's preexistence, pp. 35-37.) Abraham had not preexisted but came into existence by natural birth; therefore "was" (*genesthai*) is used of him. But "I am" designates the eternal existence of Christ apart from any idea of His ever "having come into being." And who among us will fail to relate this notable expression "I am" to the memorial name of "Jehovah" given Moses in Exodus 3:14 by the eternal God?[13] All that is in the name "I am" is to be found in Christ, the eternal Son of God.

Hebrews 13:8 testifies clearly to the eternity of Christ: "Jesus Christ the same yesterday, and to day, and for ever."

---

12. Albert Barnes, as quoted by Richard N. Davies, *The Doctrine of the Trinity*, p. 114.
13. God identified Himself to Moses by the great name "I AM THAT I AM" (Exod 3:13-15). And this very expression "I am" is recorded more than twenty times in the gospel of John as coming from the Lord's lips as a special identifying designation of Himself as the eternal God.

Richard Davies declares: "It would need no comment at all, were it not for the efforts of Unitarian writers to neutralize and destroy its force."[14] Unitarian-modernists object that the verse has no verb in it and therefore, considered by itself, has no affirmation. This argument bears no weight, for it is a well-known fact that an omission of the verb was common with the sacred writers. If we reject all passages where no verb appears, we shall have to discount many important texts, such as "God (*is*) faithful" (1 Cor 1:9); "For all men (*have*) not faith" (2 Thess 3:2); "Blessed (*is*) the man that endureth temptation" (James 1:12). There is no verb in any of these texts, but they are assuredly not to be set aside as meaningless. The subject of Hebrews 13:8 is *Jesus Christ;* and whether or not the sentence contains a verb, it declares His eternity with great positiveness.

Finally, we must note the striking declaration of Christ in Revelation 22:13: "I am the Alpha and Omega, the beginning and the end, the first and the last." His unusual designation of Himself may be traced back to Isaiah 46:10, where the sovereign God announces that He has declared "the end from the beginning" and that His counsel will stand. Only the One who is Himself the beginning and the ending could so declare the end from the beginning. When Christ says of Himself, "I am Alpha and Omega, the beginning and the end," He testifies to His own person as the eternal God. All that is involved in eternal salvation revolves around the Saviour in such a way that He is the sum and substance of God's unfolding drama. He is the God of Isaiah's prophecy, the Author and Executor of that great, comprehensive plan pointed out in Isaiah 46:10 and Ephesians 3:11. Luthardt most fittingly comments, "If He stands at the end as at the beginning, who will dare to vaunt himself in the middle?"[15]

14. Davies, p. 115.
15. Luthardt, as quoted by R. C. H. Lenski, *The Interpretation of St. John's Revelation,* p. 73.

We add the statement of Dr. Seiss as an appropriate conclusion:

> In thus appropriating them [the three designations of Christ's eternity] to Himself, the Lord Jesus Christ claims to be the eternal One, from whom all being proceeds, and to whom all being tends and returns, the source and the end of all history. He who called the world into existence, presides over all its changes, and brings it to its consummation according to His own will. He thus sets Himself before our faith as He who originated all things, who knows equally all that has happened and that will happen, and who is the ever-living and unchanging Administrator of all that is or can be, so that what He makes known as yet to take place may be accepted and relied upon with perfect confidence, as rooted and grounded in the eternal Wisdom and Almightiness. He must therefore be very God of very God, the co-equal and co-eternal Son of the Father.[16]

The truth of these words crushes all questionable and contrary views of the Lord's person and preexistence. In fact, against all liberal speculations and modernist claims that strip Him of His deity, stand the entire body of the Holy Scriptures and the true church of all ages.[17]

THE EXERCISE OF CHRIST'S MIND TOWARD HIS EQUALITY WITH GOD

The manner in which the Lord regarded His equality with

16. Joseph A. Seiss, *The Apocalypse: Lectures on the Book of Revelation,* Rev 22:13, p. 522.
17. Lenski's note is most fitting: "'All grades of kenoticism are crushed by the fact of the immutability of God, of the One Essence, which is identical in the Father, in the Son, and in the Holy Spirit. All kenoticism which subtracts attributes from God reduces deity to the nature of creatures. From a creature an attribute may be withdrawn, still leaving the creature. To withdraw even one attribute from God is to destroy God. The God who, for instance, is no longer omnipotent, is no longer God. The whole revelation of Scripture regarding God is the truth that His every attribute is His essence or being itself, revealing one side of that being. A Jesus Christ devoid of one single attribute of deity is no more the Son of God than a Jesus who on earth had only one nature, was not at all the Logos, was only Joseph's natural son" (*Epistle to the Philippians,* pp. 778-79).

the Father is described by the words "thought it not robbery" (*ouch harpagmon hēgēsato*). While this clause is somewhat difficult to interpret, it is nevertheless of great blessing and benefit to the people of God. The verb describes a "leading out before the mind" and hence means "to view, esteem, consider, count, or think." For example, in Acts 26:2 Paul says he "thinks" himself happy because of the opportunity to speak for himself before King Agrippa. Philippians 2:3 teaches believers to "esteem" each other better than themselves. In 1 Timothy 1:12, the apostle Paul renders gratitude to Christ, who, he says, "counted" him faithful. Hebrews 11:11 describes Sara's faith and states that she "judged" God faithful in His promise. In 2 Peter 1:13, Peter writes that he "thinks" it well to remind his readers of their responsibility with regard to certain great Christian virtues. The various renderings of the verb in these New Testament passages make it clear that the word denotes leadership in thought and action. It implies a mind which carefully and deliberately appraises the facts, weighs them, judges them, and determines wisely the course of conduct to be pursued.[18]

Hence, this verb reveals the character of our Lord's thinking; it shows how he valued His equality with God. His thinking did not rest solely upon inner feeling and sentiment but carefully appraised external grounds, prudently weighed and compared facts and circumstances.[19] In His delib-

18. As Kenneth S. Wuest points out: "The word translated *thought* refers to judgment based upon facts" (*Philippians in the Greek New Testament*, p. 64).

19. The verb appears in the aorist tense, thus denoting the crisis nature of Christ's thinking. It points back into the past, to a definite act of decision in His consideration of His equality with God and the great redemptive work which must be carried out. Thus it indicates the precision, positiveness, and finality with which the Lord's thinking led Him to that decision. Taken in connection with the context in verse 7, "He emptied himself," it would seem that the aorist transports us back to that time when the preexistent Son was about to come into the world by virgin birth and incarnation. He did not then, or at any other time, forcibly assert His equality with God as a means of His own self-enrichment, power and dominion, wealth and worldly glory; on the contrary, He consented to humiliation and emptied Himself for the purpose of redeeming lost men. He considered the purpose and work for which He would become man, and considered it not for Himself, but for *us*.

erate consideration we find no great solicitude for Himself. What we see filling His heart and mind and fixing His regard and concern is not what might be due to Himself, or assumed appropriately by Himself, but rather what would bring deliverance and blessedness to us. His mind held inestimable regard for others, which issued in His self-emptying.

There is nothing anywhere or at any time in history that equals the mind of Christ revealed in His self-forgetting sacrifice and devotion. His mind was the mind of God and the mind of true man; the mind of humility, love, and obedience. The mind of Christ is the wonder of the whole history of the self-emptying. The plan of redemption had its origin in His mind; that is the source of His saviourhood. *He minded to be before He became.* A worthy deliverance for the members of the fallen race, their reconciliation to God in the blessedness of eternal life—*this* was in His mind, to be secured by Him through the extremities of lowliness, obedience, and suffering. *On this His mind was set.* This was the mind of the Good Shepherd who laid down His life for His sheep. It was the mind of the Author and Finisher of our faith, who, "instead of the joy which lay before Him" (Heb 12:2, Greek), endured the cross, despising the shame. How all this was—and is—in the mind of the eternal Son of God, we are unable to conceive, but we own it to be there.

In such thinking, *He took the lead;* He has gone before to mark out the way—this great, blessed, divine pattern "who verily was foreordained before the foundation of the world, but was manifest in these last times for you" (1 Pet 1:20).

It is impossible to ignore the practical side. This great doctrinal passage is intended to reach into our minds and hearts and to draw out of us the determination to live Christ. He has marked the way for us. How can we refuse? How can our following be selfish following? This is not a divine experiment but the revelation of the will of God for His own. It is the divine will that our lives conform to the image of the

Son. Philippians 2:6 contains no grammatical comparative, but the command to conform and obey and take regard for others is too clear to be missed. The demand of this passage is for the mind of Christ to be in us so that we reflect it in our daily life and human relations. Unless we do, we are bound to be misrepresentations of Christ. We shall convey to those who look upon us a distorted impression of the One whose we are and whom we serve. It is for us to let His mind be in us, and if it *is* in us, it will not fail to show itself. The remark of Dr. Rainy is most fitting:

> Let us not separate ourselves from this fellowship of Christ; let us not be secluded from this mind of Christ. As we come to Him with our sorrows and our sins and wants, let us drink into His mind. Let us sit at His feet and learn of Him.[20]

We cannot afford to let our thinking grow careless. It is essential in days such as these that we exercise discernment, carefully appraising the external grounds, weighing and comparing the facts and circumstances before we enter into decisive action. Approving only things that are excellent is impossible without the mind which engages in careful consideration and judgment. Magnifying Christ in our bodies is impossible without the lowly, loving, obedient mind. No witness will take hold unless the mind of Christ is evident. While on the one hand, the mind of Christ will enable us to recognize error and to stand faithfully against all satanic deception, it will on the other hand also move us to humility and obedience.

The church of Christ has not been without likeness and service to her Lord. Yet the church has come far short of showing to the world the mind of Christ. The very welfare and interest of the church are involved in *this,* not in any greedy, selfish sense but from the standpoint of progress in her heavenly mission. For when the people of God let the

20. Robert Rainy, on Philippians 2:5-11, in "The Epistle to the Philippians," in *The Expositor's Bible,* 6:139.

mind of Christ rule within them, it is certain to be for their good. Things will then be right, there will be less confusion, a continuing state of revival will be present, and the way will be open to the reflecting of the image of Christ.

The most significant phrase, *ouch harpagmon*, "not a thing of grasping," remains to be considered. The word rendered "grasping" ("robbery" in the King James Version, and "a thing to be grasped" in the American Standard Version of 1901) is the chief stumbling block in the interpretation of this passage. The explanation of this great statement hinges mainly upon the meaning of this word, and it is placed forward in the sentence for emphasis, thus underscoring its importance.

Because it is a rare word, occurring only once in early literature[21] and only a few times in ecclesiastical writings, the accurate translation of the word is difficult. However, the evidence we have available, based on the usage of the word, though it is not extensive, nevertheless favors the *active* reading of the term.[22] According to the rendering of the word in its active sense of "seizing," or "grasping," the interpretation of the whole thought is this: Christ did not consider His exalted, God-equal existence a warrant for seizing, grasping to Himself the glory, exaltation, authority, afterward acquired. He might have come to earth in all the splendor and magnificence of His deity, exercising all the power and sovereignty of the Godhead, to win the homage of human hearts,

21. Plutarch *Morals* 120.
22. J. B. Gough-Pidge says: "In determining the meaning of any single word, its form is not decisive. Usage alone can decide. When usage fails to clear up the meaning, the context of the passage must be the last resort. Interpreters have generally however given the passive meaning to the word, on the ground that nouns with the termination generally denoting an action, are often used like those with the termination that denotes a result. This is undoubtedly the case here, but we have no right to assume that any noun of this class may be so used, but must furnish incontestable evidence of some example of such usage before we are justified in neglecting the obvious meaning for a less natural one, especially if the obvious meaning suits the context just as well. There is no occasion in the context to alter the significance of this word" (*Epistle to the Philippians*, p. 28).

to draw men to Himself, and to appropriate the glory, majesty, and lordship over all the earth, which were already His by virtue of His person and position, and by the divine plan. But instead of this, He did not so look upon His own things, but emptied Himself, surrendered the independent exercise of His divine attributes, and appeared in a servant's form. By way of self-denial, humiliation, and suffering, He then reached His present exalted state (vv. 9-11). Hence, the context is in full agreement with the use of this word in its active sense.[23]

We conclude, therefore, that the natural, active sense of the word is correct, and thus to be retained. Those who adhere to the passive sense of the word, that is, that the term denotes the thing seized, or grasped, rather than the act of seizing, grasping, reach in general the same result. But in order to approach that result, they make an arbitrary change in the real significance of the word. Adhering to the active sense, the interpretation is: Christ did not assert the powers of His God-given existence as warrant and authority for His own self-enrichment. He did not make use of that form and glory by appearing in all the splendor of His deity and authority to win men and to enter into His present state.[24]

So it may be said that our Lord willingly and voluntarily,

23. It is of interest to note that the noun form "robbery" is derived from the verb which means "seize, snatch away, carry off by force, claim for oneself." This verb is used by Paul in 1 Thessalonians 4:17, to describe the catching away and translation of the church saints in the rapture: those remaining alive in the earth when the Lord returns, together with those who have died in Christ and who will be resurrected, "shall be *caught up* together . . . to a meeting of the Lord in the air." The Lord, who did not seize upon His God-equal existence and use it for His own self-glory and self-enrichment, will nevertheless *lay hold upon* His saints and sweep them up in a mighty act of irresistible power, *seizing* them out and away from the earth in the rapture, for Himself.

24. In all probability, the difference between *the act of seizing* (active sense), and *the thing seized* (passive sense), is logically very small. So the God-equal existence of Christ, His powers of absolute deity, all His claims and rights of lordship and dominion earthward—all His own by virtue of who and what He is—and His determination not to assert those powers, prerogatives, and indefeasible rights, in order to high-handedly enrich Himself, are very closely and logically related.

after weighing the facts, and not for a moment even contemplating the possibility of such selfish and forceful means by which to grasp for Himself, after becoming man, the power, dominion, wealth, and glory already His by His own Godhead, waived those rights and claims for the accomplishment of an infinite, eternal purpose, namely, the fulfillment of the work of redemption for mankind. As verses 7 and 8 show so clearly, He took His lot as a man among men and chose the way of humiliation and self-abasement, which necessarily led to the ignominious death on a cross. Thus it was that He said to Andrew and Philip: "Except a corn of wheat fall into the ground and die, it abideth alone; but if it die, it bringeth forth much fruit . . . but for this cause came I unto this hour" (John 12:24-27). As He stood before Pilate, He said: "To this end was I born, and for this cause came I into the world, that I should bear witness unto the truth. Every one that is of the truth heareth my voice" (John 18:37). The purpose may be summed up in this: "And without controversy great is the mystery of godliness: God was manifest in the flesh, justified in the Spirit, seen of angels, preached unto the Gentiles, believed on in the world, received up into glory" (1 Tim 3:16).

We may let the words of verse 6 be taken in conclusion, since they deal irrefutably with the fact of the deity of Christ. First, there is the statement of the great truth concerning the *preexistence* of Christ: He existed in the "form of God." Then follows the declaration with respect to the *person* of Christ: He "was equal with God." Third, we have a revelation of the *posture* of Christ's mind: He counted not His equality with God a treasure to be selfishly used to enrich Himself. Finally, extending the compass of the statement into verse 7 (NASB), to complete the thought, we note the *position* which He took when He came into the world to fulfill the redemptive purpose: He "emptied Himself, taking the form of a . . . [slave]."

The treasures of this passage have not been exhausted by any means, even when these truths have been drawn from it.

For who can probe exhaustively into the glory and humiliation of our Lord Jesus Christ? I have not done it in this book,
nor could all the books or all the minds in this world. The
magnitude, magnificence, and mystery of these verses cannot
be circumscribed by reason or logic. But they can be ap-
proached and accepted by faith. As Bishop Moule once wrote,
"This is not in the least a controversial assertion. It is simply
part of an argument to the heart."[25] Paul appeals to believers
from several motives, but then he brings in the greatest of
them all: "Let this mind be in you, which was also in Christ
Jesus" (v. 5). Here at once is the great motive, mind, and
model for all the saints. The mind of the Head must be the
mind of His body. We must "walk in love, as Christ also hath
loved us" (Eph 5:2). He did not count His equality with God
as something to be used selfishly for His own enrichment. To
hold by this was not the great object for Him. The Son of God
might well have aimed at maintaining and disclosing that
equality with God—that alternative was open. But this is
not what we behold; no such motive, no solicitude about that
appears. His subsequent procedure, His actions, His words,
reveal nothing of this kind. Rather, we see Him coming down
to act in *our* behalf, to deliver *us,* to bring the blessing of salvation to *us.* This is the basis of the Scripture appeal to us
that we "should follow his steps" (1 Pet 2:21). All Christians
are thus enjoined to renounce the selfish consideration of their
own rights, claims, and prerogatives.

This sounds the death knell upon the erroneous idea that
doctrine and duty do not go together. It pronounces the in-
dictment of the fallacy of religious thought which dismisses
Christian doctrine as being too antiquated for this modern
age. Christian doctrine is the catena of eternal and vital facts
set forth by means of the Holy Scriptures, that we may live
by them and in obedience to them. This great passage before
us is Holy Scripture, filled and charged to the brim with the

25. H. C. G. Moule, *Philippian Studies,* pp. 101-2.

person, natures, and work of Christ. And it is all in order that believers tempted by the worldliness of this age to a life of self-interest and self-assertion might instead "look . . . on the things of others" (Phil 2:4). The reason for this is that our blessed Lord did in fact think and act precisely in this way for His own. Without the doctrinal facts set forth by inspiration in the record of the Word of God, all these appeals to us would be nothing more than mere rhetoric, without any motive and lever for the affections and the will. As Moule wrote:

> Oh reason of reasons, argument of arguments—the Lord Jesus Christ! Nothing in Christianity lies really outside of Him. His person and His work embody all its dogmatic teaching. His example, His love "which passeth knowledge" is the sum and life of all its morality.[26]

The Word of God teaches the supreme and absolute deity of the Lord Jesus Christ with such simplicity and force as to place it beyond all doubt. The true church of Jesus Christ believes it and rests solidly upon it. While the Holy Scriptures are the great, final, and infallible proof, yet perhaps the most practical proof of Christ's deity to the believer rests in his own inner relationship *to*, experience *of*, and fellowship *with* the Lord of glory. The born-again Christian has in his own heart the living certainty of the deity of Christ. The believer experiences daily answers to prayer; transformation of life which issues in nobler motives, increase in faith, and growth in grace; together with the inspiration and motivation drawn from the influence of the One who dwells within him— the One who is Himself Lord, the supreme object of faith and hope: "Christ in you, the hope of glory" (Col 1:27*b*).

Here, then, is the place where we stand. Here our faith is anchored. It is the *living Lord* abiding in us, who guards our hearts and minds. He is our Lord and our God. Fitting indeed is the closing statement of B. B. Warfield, in his inspiring essay on the deity of Christ:

26. Moule, p. 104.

The supreme proof to every Christian of the deity of Christ is then his own inner experience of the transforming power of his Lord upon the heart and life. Not more surely does he who feels the present warmth of the sun know that the sun exists, than he who has experienced the re-creative power of the Lord knows Him to be his Lord and his God. Here is perhaps, we may say, the proper, certainly we must say, the most convincing proof to every Christian, of the deity of Christ; a proof which he cannot escape, and to which, whether he is capable of analyzing it or drawing it out in logical statement or not, he cannot fail to yield his sincere and unassailable conviction. Whatever else he may or may not be assured of, he knows that his Redeemer lives. Because He lives, the believer lives also—that is the ineradicable conviction of every Christian heart.[27]

27. Benjamin B. Warfield, "The Deity of Christ," in *The Fundamentals,* 3:245-46.

3

THE INCARNATION OF CHRIST

*But made himself of no reputation, and took upon
him the form of a servant, and was made in the likeness of men* (Phil 2:7).

The reader will note at once the point of contrast in the
connection between verses 6 and 7. Christ did not regard His
equality with God as a prize to be selfishly grasped, or as a
treasure to be kept for personal self-enrichment; but on the
contrary, He made Himself of no reputation, that is, He "emptied Himself." Since Christ was truly God, it would not be
arrogance on His part to claim equality of nature with God.
But He, although He was truly God, did not make a point of
retaining the advantages connected with His divine state of
being. In any steps He might take, in any actions He might
engage, in any forthgoings He might enter on, the Son of God
might have aimed at maintaining and manifesting His equality with God. That alternative was open to Him. But this is
not what we see. But what we do see filling His heart and
fixing His regard is not what might be due to Himself but
what would bring deliverance and blessedness to *us*. Laying
aside the divine, glorious form which, before His incarnation,
was the form of appearance of His God-equal existence, He
assumed the form of a bondslave, and became in the likeness
of men, for the great purpose set forth in verse 8.

The following chart of verses 7 and 8, which outlines the
experience of Christ in the different phases, sets forth the facts

of the passage and can be used in assembling and understanding those facts.

CONTENT OF THE PASSAGE:	CHARACTER OF THE ACT REVEALED AS:	CONDUCT OF CHRIST INVOLVES:
Self-emptying (v. 7a)	Surrender	Submission
Servanthood (v. 7b)	Servility	Service
Saviourship (v. 7c)	Sinlessness	Suffering
Sacrifice (v. 8)	Substitution	Salvation

THE ACT OF SELF-EMPTYING

Of the many words and expressions that are used in the
New Testament to describe the incarnation of the Lord Jesus
Christ, "But He emptied Himself" are perhaps the most outstanding. It is not difficult to find words to describe the entrance into human existence of an ordinary man; the common
man is conceived and born. This is the origin, or beginning,
of his existence. But it is not so easy to describe the entrance
into the world of One such as our Lord. The New Testament
writers were faced with the necessity for finding and using
words to describe—not the beginning of Christ's personal existence—but the entrance into human life of One who had
existed from all eternity. The writers of the New Testament,
under inspiration, almost exhaust the resources of human language in their effort to emphasize the great fact that Christ's
coming into the world was different than the entrance into
human existence of ordinary men.

The portal of Christ's entrance into the world was the virgin
birth, by which the preexistent Son of God became incarnate
in human flesh, form, and nature. He became true man, yet at
the same time He never ceased to be God. He who gave form

to all things, and Himself set the type of what was highest and best in the universe, transcending meanwhile all created excellence in His uncreated glory, is seen conforming Himself to the type, or model, of the likeness of one of His creatures, man. He came into human existence as men do, but by the special and miraculous power of the Holy Spirit replacing the procreative human process. He continued in that state of human existence, yet it is not said that He was merely man or had become nothing but a man. He was in "the likeness of men," and was "found in fashion as a man." He is truly God and truly man, back in the place of glory and Godhead, having risen from the dead and ascended into the heavenly habitation of God. He has won the victory over evil and secured the redemption of His people. Having assumed the form and nature of man, He has returned to the heavenly place where, as man, He is again clothed with all the glory of God and is seated at His Father's right hand.

In taking the great step of assuming the form of a servant and becoming in fashion as a man, He "emptied Himself" (NASB; "made himself of no reputation," KJV). The most logical and apparent meaning of this statement indicates an emptying, not of something which Christ did not at first have but might assume, but rather, of something He already possessed. The emptying seems by design to be contrasted with the thought of accumulation of self-enrichment contained in the clause "thought it not robbery to be equal with God." Christ emptied Himself, surrendering the "form of God," and assumed the servile abasement of the "form of a servant."

Writers and commentators have greatly extended themselves in attempting to explain this classical statement of Christ's humiliation. Certain erroneous views, which are positive denials of either Christ's deity or His true humanity, or both, have been widely advocated. The Unitarian expositors, together with current modernist leaders and liberal theologians, actively reject the fact of the two natures in the one person of Jesus Christ, and so deny the truth of this great passage. However, their false allegations may be refuted by a simple, accurate, scriptural exegesis of the passage. It seems most certain that the expression "He emptied Himself" cannot mean that He who was with God, and who was God, could renounce His essential nature and cease to be God. A contradiction like this involves the mind in darkness and is most assuredly excluded by the Scriptures. The One who came into the world to dwell among men is Immanuel, "God with us." We must be careful not to take anything away from the testimony of this great passage. Our Lord Jesus Christ, in becoming man, entered into the experience of human limitation, human weakness and impoverishment, human dependence, and human subjection. This was in singular contrast with the glory and plenitude He possessed in the form of God.

So here, by contrast, our attention is fixed upon His incarnation—the act of His self-emptying. This emptying draws our greatest regard and wonder. Instead of the form of God, there rises before us this true human history of God's Son, this lowly manhood, and it took place by His emptying Himself. But we must ever keep in mind that in this act of humiliation and servility, He did not thrust aside and renounce His Godhead.[1]

In what did this act of self-emptying consist? First, it consisted negatively, in the Lord's preexistent state, of a free and willing determination not to hold fast His equality with God. Second, it then consisted, in the positive sense, with regard to His historical existence, in His emptying Himself, taking the form of a bondslave, being made in the likeness of men.

1. Compare the works of such writers as Dorner, Ebrard, Wernle, Zahn, Channing, Farley, Beecher, Bennett, Bultmann, Braun, Fosdick, Ferre, Marxen, Conzelman, Mezger, and Hartmann as representatives of those who reject the biblical teaching of the incarnation of Christ. On the other hand, many notable interpreters, past and present, have ably defended the deity and true humanity of Christ in the kenosis passage, although differing somewhat in their manner of expressing the act denoted by the words "He emptied Himself." See the writings of Westcott, Lightfoot, Alford, Lange, Ellicott, Strong, Vincent, Thayer, Davies, Rainy, Morgan, Wuest, Hoyt, Lenski, and others.

As Bruce remarks, "The Son of God took human nature that He might, as a man, live in the form of a servant."[2]

But we do well to remember that His self-emptying for our salvation involves realities which we cannot conceive of or put into adequate words. He emptied Himself in becoming man. Here is the eminent example of a great divine mystery which, being revealed, remains a mystery never to be adequately explained, and yet which proves full of meaning and power. The Word was made flesh. The very One through whom all the universe took form and being, walked about Judea in the lowliness of that practical, historic manhood. We cannot explain this in so many words; it is the wonder of the eternal God. But to believe it in our hearts makes all things become new for us. The meaning it has for human history and mankind is inexhaustible.

Those who have steadfastly defended the virgin birth and incarnation of Christ have expressed themselves in varied manner on the subject of Christ's self-emptying. For example, Lightfoot says, "He stripped Himself of the insignia of majesty by taking the form of a slave." Thayer interprets: "He laid aside equality with, or the form of God, so as to assume the form of a slave." Davies states: "He did not lay aside, lose, or relinquish the divine attributes when He became man, but refused to use them for His own safety, welfare, and glory." Morgan comments: "He did not lay aside the essential facts of His deity, He simply changed the form of His manifestation . . . and there came into existence a person in all points human, in all essentials divine." Lenski remarks: "His full deity remained." Wuest writes: "When our Lord set aside the expression of deity in order that He might express Himself as a bondslave, He was setting aside His legitimate and natural desires and prerogatives as deity."

I prefer the interpretation of Strong and Hoyt, who say:

2. A. B. Bruce, *The Humiliation of Christ,* p. 20.

the humiliation expressed by the verb "emptied" consisted in the giving up of the independent exercise of the divine attributes.

Strong writes:

> The divine in Christ during most of His earthly life, is latent, or only now and then . . . manifested to others. . . . What the Logos divested Himself of, in becoming man, is not the substance of his Godhead, but the "form of God" in which this substance was manifested. This "form of God" can be only that independent exercise of the powers and prerogatives of Deity which constitutes his "equality with God."[3]

This view places the emphasis upon the adjective "independent," and is most satisfactory and explanatory.

It is in fine harmony with the interpretation we believe must be applied to the phrase "form of God" discussed earlier. It allows for all the manifestations of divine power and knowledge which are so evident during the Lord's earthly ministry, as the gospels clearly attest, and still does not eliminate the doctrine of a real kenosis.

The comprehensive outline of this view given by Dr. A. H. Strong in his *Systematic Theology* is most helpful to our understanding of the correct interpretation of the self-emptying.[4] For that reason I present a paraphrase of the outline at this point. It is not lengthy, and is certain to be of great benefit to us in our grasp of the truth of this extraordinary statement. Strong suggests that the humiliation of Christ, as the Scriptures show, consisted:

1. In the act of the preexistent Son of God by which He gave up His divine glory with the Father in order to take a

---

3. A. H. Strong, *Systematic Theology*, pp. 705-6. Strong's initial statement with reference to Christ's self-humiliation is: "We may distinguish: (a) That act of the preincarnate Logos by which, in becoming man, he gave up the independent exercise of the divine attributes" (p. 704). Herman A. Hoyt says, "The self-emptying consists in the surrender of the independent use of His attributes" (Lecture notes on the Epistle to the Philippians, Grace Theological Seminary, Winona Lake, Ind., 1943).

4. Strong, pp. 703-4.

servant's form. In this act He resigned not the possession of the divine attributes, nor entirely their use, but rather the independent exercise of those attributes (John 17:5; Phil 2:6-7; 2 Cor 8:9).

2. In the submission of the Son to the control of the Holy Spirit and the limitations of His Messianic mission, in His communication of the divine fullness of the human nature which He had taken into union with Himself (Acts 1:2; 10:38; Heb 9:14).

3. In the Son's continuous surrender so far as His human nature was concerned, of the independent use of those attributes and divine powers with which that human nature was endowed by virtue of its union with the divine, and in the voluntary acceptance, which followed upon this, of temptation, suffering, and death (Matt 26:53; John 10:17-18; Phil 2:8).

Each of these points has scriptural support. We must therefore regard the humiliation of Christ not as consisting only in the act of self-emptying, but as involving a continuous self-renunciation, which began with the kenosis of the Son of God in becoming man, and which culminated in the self-subjection of the God-man to the death of a cross. In the process of unfolding the complexity of the self-emptying, our hearts climb to new heights of gratitude and appreciation for the blessed Saviour's work. How can we remain unmoved in the fact of such unsurpassed love?

We shall consider the exposition of the statement "He emptied Himself," or as the King James Version renders it, He "made himself of no reputation," in a series of ten inter-related exegetical points, each of which is in itself most significant. Even then, however, it is not possible for the finite mind to probe the depths of the great heart of Him who, while stooping to manhood, was essentially divine. Notwithstanding, the following ten points constitute an endeavor to help readers understand this stupendous act of Christ, which is of such great and vital significance to His true church.

1. The passage does not state that Christ *emptied out of Himself* the form of God, nor of His equality with God. Neither does the passage state that our Lord *exchanged* the form of God for the form of a slave, nor for the likeness of men.

2. The statement "but He emptied Himself" is, in itself, an incomplete thought, leaving us with the question, Of what did He empty Himself? The Holy Spirit, through the apostle, answers the question and thus completes the thought, not by stating that Christ emptied out of Himself anything He had previously possessed, but by describing the nature of the humiliation: "took upon him the form of a servant, and was made in the likeness of men."

3. The sense of "emptied" (*ekenōsen*) is pressed by the liberal theologians until nothing of deity is left. They insist that the verb must be held to its literal meaning of "empty out the contents," thus proving that Christ emptied out of Himself all the attributes and essentialities of deity. Such a view impugns the holy Trinity. For if Christ emptied out of Himself all the qualities of deity, then He ceased to be God, and there was no Son, no eternal Word, no Trinity. While the verb does have the meaning of "empty" in the Greek writings, in none of the eight places where it appears in the Scriptures does it designate emptying a subject of its contents.[5] So the Unitarian-modernist insistence on the literality of "emptied" loses its force, and the use and meaning of the word in the Scriptures constitute instead a refutation of the view

5. It is found three times in the Septuagint: Nehemiah 5:13 ("emptied"); Jeremiah 14:2; 15:9 ("languisheth"), where the sense is clearly "abase, to be poor and lowly, humble." The word occurs four times besides the text, in the New Testament: Romans 4:14 ("made void"), 1 Corinthians 1:17 ("made of none effect"), where its signification is plainly "to deprive of force, render useless," and in 1 Corinthians 9:15 ("void") and 2 Corinthians 9:3 ("be in vain"), where it obviously means "to cause a thing to be seen as vain, hypocritical, false."

that Christ emptied Himself of all the qualities and attributes of deity.

McClain remarks:

> He could not, as some suggest, have actually surrendered
> the divine attributes, for they are functions potential in the
> very nature of God. Granted that the *active* functioning
> might cease for a time, still the *potentiality* remains. To sug-
> gest this might also be given up is to say that God may cease
> to be God. But such an idea is repugnant to reason, and
> surely cannot be discovered in the Scriptures. On the con-
> trary, our Lord, during the days of His flesh, very definitely
> asserts His possession of divine power when, referring to the
> laying down of His life, He declares: "I have power to lay it
> down, and I have power to take it again." It will not do
> either, to say as others have said, that the Son gave up the
> use of His divine attributes during the period of His earthly
> life, though if interpreted rightly this statement might be
> accepted as a true account. It is better to say with Dr.
> Strong, that Christ gave up the *independent use* of His di-
> vine attributes.[6]

The related view that Christ gave up certain relative attributes such as omniscience, omnipotence, and omnipresence, is also clearly refuted, since this theory leads to a further
denial of the possession of any divine attributes, or of any divine consciousness at all on the part of Christ.[7] To give up
any of the divine attributes is to give up the substance of the
Godhead, and with Strong we say, "Nor is it a sufficient reply
to say that only the relative attributes are given up, while
the immanent attributes, which chiefly characterize the God-

6. Alva J. McClain, "The Doctrine of the Kenosis in Philippians 2:5-8,"
The Biblical Review 13 (October 1928):507.

7. It is of the utmost importance that we understand this. For the very
mildest kenotic view that Christ, prior to His incarnation, or afterward, gave
up even one of His attributes of deity, means that the Son by His own act,
ceased to be God. To empty out one attribute destroys the deity of the Son
as completely as to empty out of Him *all* the attributes.

head, are retained; for the immanent necessarily involve the relative, as the greater involve the less."[8]

4. The verb "emptied" (*ekenōsen*) is the aorist active indicative form, denoting that the work of self-emptying was a definite, crisis act on the part of Christ. He was not acted upon; no other force or power prevailed over Him to induce the self-emptying. It was a voluntary, determinate act, which initiated the self-imposed humiliation and issued in the atoning death on the cross. Thus any idea of a process of mere self-forgetfulness in the human life of the Lord is completely obviated. This is a simple and effective refutation of the theory that Christ's humiliation was merely an experience that took place in the outward trials, sorrows, and privations of His earthly life.

5. The verbal expression "emptied," while designating the crisis act of Christ's divesting Himself, is nevertheless guarded and supported by the two following clauses, "took the form of a slave" and "was made in the likeness of men." Bruce says, "The first clause declares the end of the incarnation, the second sets forth the incarnation itself as the means to that end."[9] The carefulness of the Holy Spirit in the selection of the language, to show how the emptying was accomplished and in what it consisted, is indeed striking. Christ divested Himself of the independent exercise of His attributes, assuming a slave's form, and took the nature of men, as suggested by the terms "form" and "likeness," but neither to empty out His divine nature and thus divest Himself of it, nor to exchange that divine nature for a slave's form. The greatest caution and direction have been exercised here to preserve the text from error and to insure against the very theories adopted by some, which dispense with both the deity and true humanity of Christ.

6. The clauses "being in the form of God" and "to be equal

8. Strong, pp. 701-2.
9. Bruce, p. 20.

with God" of verse 6 clearly establish the eternal preexistence and deity of Christ. Our blessed Lord is God, to which all Scripture testifies. Since *He is God*, His nature, attributes, and will are completely exempt from all change. Men change every day, the creation changes, energy is spent, and motion characterizes the tiniest particle just as surely as it does the immense solar system. But God does not change. Both reason and the Holy Scriptures attest this fact. Strong writes:

> Reason teaches us that no change is possible in God, whether of increase and decrease, progress or deterioration, contraction or development. All change must be to better or to worse. But God is absolute perfection, and no change to better is possible. Change to worse would be equally inconsistent with perfection. No cause for such change exists, either outside of God, or in God Himself.[10]

The Scriptures state: "Thou art the same" (Psalm 102:27); "I, Jehovah, change not" (Mal 3:6, ASV); "Jesus Christ the same yesterday, and to day, and for ever" (Heb 13:8). Thus it is impossible for Christ to cease to be God, to divest Himself of any or all of His attributes, to empty out of Himself His essential nature, or even to exchange it for another, at any time. The self-emptying must conform with this fact; hence, it does not, cannot, teach that our Lord surrendered, laid aside, exchanged, emptied out, or divested Himself of His deity or of any part of it.

7. The expression "emptied Himself" is further described as "taking a bondslave's form," literally with the aorist participle: "having taken a bondslave's form." By "form" is meant not mere external semblance but characteristic attributes, as with "form" in verse 6. Thus the "form of a bondslave" was real, not the sham human nature insisted upon by some nor the fleshly substance without a human soul advocated by certain others. That Christ's humanity was true and genuine, in

10. Strong, p. 257.

that He possessed the essential elements of human nature, material body and rational soul, is clearly taught in the Scriptures. Three passages illustrate this truth: John 8:40, "Ye seek to kill me, a man that hath told you the truth"; 1 Timothy 2: 5, "One mediator between God and man, the man Christ Jesus"; and Hebrews 2:14, "Forasmuch then as the children are partakers of flesh and blood, he also himself took part of the same."

8. With regard to the phrase "emptied Himself," it may be said that only God could limit Himself, that is, only He Himself could give up the independent exercise of His attributes. This is supported by the emphatic position of the pronoun "Himself" in the sentence, which indicates that the humiliation was voluntarily self-imposed. Thus the self-emptying is a guarantee that Christ is God the Son.

9. It should also be said that the testimony of the whole passage decisively precludes that in *emptying Himself,* Christ only acted as though He did not possess the divine attributes. Such a view makes Christ the perpetrator of a gigantic hoax, and must be dismissed as unworthy of serious consideration, except to show its falsity by citing John 17:3, "the only true God," and John 14:6, "I am . . . the truth." Truth is an immanent attribute of Christ, an active characteristic of His eternal being. He can do nothing contrary to His own nature. Therefore, to pretend that He did not possess His attributes would have been to act entirely unlike Himself and to contradict His own character of truth. This He could not do.

10. Finally, we may say that Christ, the Son, existed in the form of God, coequal and coeternal with the Father, clothed with all the glories of deity manifested in external form. He had all the nature of the true God, but did not count this state of equality with God, and the power and glory thereof, as something to be grasped and used as a means to self-enrichment. Instead, He lovingly condescended to give up the independent use of His attributes of deity, and to stoop down

to assume a servant form, and become man by virgin birth and incarnation. As a result of this act, His entire earthly life and experience as true man became the life and experience of a bondslave. Throughout the entire span of this earthly life the Lord never acted, never spoke, never assumed anything *of or by Himself, independently of the Father.* He was at all times under the power and direction of the Father through the presence and ministry of the Holy Spirit. There was, then, a limitation upon the exercise of the great divine attributes in connection with His stooping down from the form of God to the form of a servant. McClain states:

> In this sense, during His earthly sojourn, the "external glory" was utterly laid aside. "He was in the world, and the world was made by Him, and the world knew Him not." But there was another, an inner glory; and this glory, of which the external glory had been indicative, was still present, though veiled by the servant-form. He did not—it is not too much to say that He could not—empty Himself of this. And to those who came to know Him because their eyes were enlightened by the Spirit, His blessed inner glory became apparent in spite of the veil of the flesh, so that they could witness that "The Word became flesh, and dwelt among us (and we beheld His glory, the glory as of the Only-begotten of the Father), full of grace and truth."[11]

THE ASSUMPTION OF SERVANTHOOD

"Having taken the form of a servant" is a continuation of the whole thought beginning with "who, being in the form of God" in verse 6, and shows us the *method* of the self-emptying. There is no connective word *and* in the original text, the presence of which would tend to convey the idea that there are three separate acts set forth in the sentence. However, both of the following clauses in verse 7 are parts of the modal definition of "He emptied Himself." They do not describe actions that are separate and distinct from the self-emptying.

11. McClain, p. 520.

The verbal expression "took" in the King James Version is the second aorist participle from the verb *lambanō* (take, receive), laying stress upon that which is taken or received. The aorist tense of the verb points to the historic event of Christ's taking a bondslave's form, and describes the definite and effective move on the part of the Lord . The action of this aorist participle "took" (KJV), literally, "having taken," is coincident in time with the action in "emptied Himself," although it is subordinate in thought. So also is the aorist participle "was made" (KJV) in the last clause. So all these aorist verbal expressions point to the same crisis act when Christ divested Himself of the independent use of His divine attributes and became man.

In emptying Himself, then, Christ assumed "a bondslave's form." As every creature is in absolute subjection to God's authority and to His providence, so Christ came to be. He entered into a discipline of subjection and obedience. In verse 6, He appears in His preincarnate state, in the form of God, equal with God, expressing Himself as Deity. In verse 7, the same Christ appears in His incarnation, having not emptied out of Himself His deity, His God-equal existence, yet now expressing Himself as a bondslave. The aorist participle "having taken" shows us that He did not in that manner express Himself in His preincarnate state, although the purpose and desire to serve others were a real part of His nature and character of deity.

The word "servant" (KJV) means literally "bondslave." The noun "bondslave" stands without the definite article, thus indicating character, kind, and quality, rather than a specific slave. It enlarges on the word "form" and shows how the word reveals the concern for mankind in the great, eternal heart of our Lord, and His purpose and intent for their redemption. It speaks of a servile relationship to another, a giving of oneself to another's will, and a reciprocal bond of love. Christ manifested all these characteristics in His relationship

The Incarnation of Christ

to God the Father. The word shows the lowliness, humbleness, and subservience of the form which Christ assumed to minister to others. The One who is Lord and Master of all became the slave of all.[12] The Lord Himself said, "And whosoever will be chief among you, let him be your servant [bondslave]: even as the Son of man came not to be ministered unto, but to minister, and to give his life a ransom for many" (Matt 20:27-28).[13]

How unintimidating a servant is. We all appreciate the service of a loyal slave, yet none of us aspire to become one. It is a role which no one desires to assume. So God Himself took it and ministered among us, and loved us, and showed us bodily what kind of life we could enjoy linked with Him through the Holy Spirit.

The work of redemption was accomplished by God in servant form. If He had not taken such a form, He could not have wrought our salvation. Hebrews 10:5-10 says, "But a body hast thou prepared me . . . Lo, I come . . . to do thy will, O God. . . . By the which will we are sanctified through the offering of the body of Jesus Christ once for all." If He had

12. McClain points out: "When He took upon Him servant-form, the Son of God came to be the *perfect* servant, to reveal the ideal servanthood. But the perfect servant must render a *perfect* service. Not many will care to affirm that our Lord failed at this point. He Himself said: 'I do nothing of myself, but as the Father taught me, I speak these things. And He that hath sent me is with me; He hath not left me alone; for I do always the things that are pleasing to Him.' (Jn. 8:28-29). And again: 'For I speak not from myself, but the Father that sent me, He hath given me commandment, what I should say, and what I should speak' (Jn. 12:49). 'Which of you convicteth me of sin?' (Jn. 8:46). There is no room for fallibility here, whatever view we may take of Christ's humiliation. On the contrary as Bishop Moule has pointed out, the kenosis itself becomes the *guarantee* of His infallibility. Whatever He was before entrance into human existence, by His self-emptying, He becomes the perfect bondservant of Jehovah, who does nothing and speaks nothing from Himself, but speaks only what the Father commands, and does always the things that are pleasing to Him. Therefore, in the days of His flesh, the Son of Man may be trusted without reserve in every statement He has been pleased to make, for His words are in every instance the very words of God" (McClain, p. 508).

13. Strong comments, "The form of God can only be that independent exercise of the powers and prerogatives of Deity which constitutes His equality with God. This He surrenders, in the act of taking the form of a servant— or, becoming subordinate, as a man" (p. 706).

descended to earth only in that form seen by His apostles on the mount of transfiguration, the whole redemptive purpose—the incarnation, life, suffering, death, and resurrection, as recorded in the Holy Word—would not have been accomplished.

Not only the form of His servanthood but also the service performed by the One in that form was portrayed by the prophet Isaiah in unmistakable lines seven hundred years before the incarnation. In Isaiah 42:1, the voice of God is heard to say through the prophet: "Behold my servant, whom I uphold." And the Servant's mission is set forth in verses 6 and 7: "for a light of the Gentiles; to open the blind eyes, to bring out the prisoners from the prison, and them that sit in darkness out of the prison house."

The same prophet had first announced the virgin birth and incarnation of the One of whose servanthood he later spoke, and had declared the manner by which the Saviour would appear in a servant's form: "Behold, a [lit., "the"] virgin shall conceive, and bear a son, and shall call his name Immanuel" (Isa 7:14). To the Hebrews, "Immanuel" was a descriptive name, and the simple meaning was "God with us." All this was the distinct foretelling of the stupendous fact of the descent of God the Son to earth, to appear in a slave's form.

But when He came, even with His humble entrance into human life, there was no welcome for Him, among Jew, Roman, or Greek. "He was in the world, and the world was made by him, and the world knew him not" (John 1:10). The world was in turmoil, and corruption was everywhere, "and that in spite of the best men could do in government, in culture, and in religion."[14] Men had become enveloped in the materialism of the age, had generally lost their spiritual sense, and had no conception of a lowly and suffering Saviour who would come to save them from their sins. But while neither expected nor desired, nevertheless He came, appearing in a slave's form, because in God's economy the time was ripe for

14. G. Campbell Morgan, *The Crises of the Christ,* p. 97.

His advent into the world, a world where men had sunk to the deepest depths in sin and had departed far from the true God.

But out of the world there were some who received Him, and "as many as received him, to them gave he power to become . . . [children] of God, even to them that believe in his name" (John 1:12). So it has been through the centuries. In the lowly Servant, men have found the way, the truth, and the life. In the One who emptied Himself, divested Himself of the independent use of His attributes, and appeared on earth in the form of a slave, men have found their way back to God, from whom they were alienated by their sins. In every generation, *some* have received Him in His slave's form, and have thus passed from death to life.

It is serious error to pass over the practical teaching of our Lord's servanthood. A bondslave waits on others, works for the interests of others, attends to the needs of others. A bondslave is bound to serve others. The place of a slave is a lowly place, yet one of dignity because of the motive involved and the service required. Our Lord took this place, assumed this form—He stooped to slavehood—willingly, voluntarily, to raise us to the dignity of adult children, sons and kings; and in His subsequent exaltation (Phil 2:9-11), we see the pledge and certainty that are ours. Godhead was His by right, slavehood His by a free act. It is unequaled, unsurpassed, in all the annals of men. It was said of Him, "Never man spake like this man" (John 7:46). It may also, with like sacredness and verity, be said of Him, "Never man *served* like this man."

The failure that threatens is that we who receive Him as our Saviour do not love and honor Him as Lord and as our supreme standard for daily living; that we refuse to pattern our living by His, our minds by His. Modernism falsely accepts Him only as an example, holds Him to be mere man and nothing more, discounting His deity and incarnation. But the testimony of the Scriptures is clear: the Christ of God came down into the realm of men, to save us from our sins by a wondrous but terrible emptying, humbling, and sacrifice of Himself. Not only did He redeem us, but He left for all the redeemed a pattern of life, the Christian standard for all those born again from above, for all ages. It is obvious, therefore, that the life of the saved, patterned after His, will be a life of self-emptying, surrender, submission to the blessed Lord Jesus Christ, and the acknowledgment of His lordship. It cannot be other than this. If it conforms to His example, it must be a life of slavehood, servility, and service performed in His strength, with His enablement, and with His honor and glory in mind. It will be a life of service done for Him, for others, because of love, because we have realized the divine purpose in our presence on earth among men: "to abide in the flesh is more needful *for you*" (Phil 1:24, italics added). To serve Him, then, means sacrifice and self-denial on our part, and a desire for the advantage, help, enlightenment, and edification of others. Our life on earth as true Christians is that of love that cannot be denied: "And walk in love, as Christ also hath loved us, and hath given himself for us" (Eph 5:2).

The Abasement of Saviourship

"Having become in the likeness of men" is the simple, precise declaration of the Lord's true humanity. Yet in simplicity there is strength. No words can better express how wonderful it is that our Lord should be so found. His humanity was the necessary medium through which Christ was to express Himself as a bondslave, servant of mankind. The *fact* of His becoming man is set specifically before us by the phrase "having become in likeness of men." In doing so, many great interests fell to Him to be cared for, not in the manner of Godhead, which speaks and it is done, but with the labor, lowliness, pain, and suffering of a faithful bond servant. He said to the rulers and religious leaders who opposed and rejected

Him and His mission: "The Father which sent me, he gave me a commandment" (John 12:49). And He had to carry out that command. He did so as true man. While "having become in likeness of men" specifies His true humanity, the whole statement, "But He emptied Himself, having taken a slave's form, having been made in likeness of men," is a grand expression of the incarnation.

Thus, having set forth the great fact of Christ's incarnation, the passage flows on into the climax of the whole thought begun in verse 5—the self-abasement of the eternal Son of God for our redemption. It was His mind to not selfishly consider and make use of His God-equal existence for His own self-interest, but rather to give up the independent use of His divine attributes, taking a slave's form in that He became in men's likeness. In fashion found as man, He lowered Himself and became obedient to the accursed death of a cross. All this He did voluntarily, never turning back, prompted by His own unutterable love. This is the great purpose of "having become in likeness of men."

The act of self-abasement is designated by the words "was made" (KJV).[15] This verb is the same as that used in John 1:14 to designate the fact that the Word *became* flesh, and the two passages refer to the same act of incarnation. Our Lord entered into a new state of being when He became man, a state that was necessary for the redemption of mankind. He Himself must become a man in order to die on the cross for our sins. So, by a miraculous creative act in the womb of the virgin Mary, He became incarnate in human flesh (John 1:14), in that body "prepared" for Him (Heb 10:5). In be-

---

15. The form of the verb rendered "was made" in the King James Version, is the aorist participle of *ginomai*, "to come into existence, come to pass, become, take place." It is rendered "to be made" in the sense of *who* or *what* a person or thing is or has been made, expressed in terms of character, quality, condition, place, or rank. The aorist participle signifies entrance into a new state, and denotes what was contemporaneous with the Lord's emptying Himself. His becoming in the likeness of men was simultaneous with His emptying Himself, part of that act but subordinate to it.

coming man, our Lord Jesus Christ brought that which cannot be limited into the realm of the limited; He came from
the infinite to the finite.

Morgan says, "The Word passed from government to obedience, from independent cooperation in the equality of deity,
to dependent submission to the will of God."[16] This is precisely what took place. It is a mystery that eludes final and complete explanation. Yet it is a mystery revealed, upon which
the whole structure of the Christian faith depends. The Scriptures state *the fact*, and almost exhaust the resources of human language in expressing that fact and in emphasizing the
difference between Christ's entrance into human life and
that of ordinary men. The people of God should take special
notice of this in reading their Bibles and studying the truth of
the incarnation as it is set forth in the Scriptures. By way of
the incarnation there entered into a new state of being a person in all points human, but in all essentials divine. He was,
without doubt, true man, yet He did not cease to be God in
becoming man. McClain remarks:

> To the New Testament writers Christ is a real man made
> "in all things like unto His brethren," yet we are not to for-
> get there is a difference: we are sinners, but He is "holy,
> guileless, undefiled, separated from sinners." Aside from this
> there is no limit in His kenosis. He became partaker of flesh
> and blood; is born of a woman under the law; grows in wis-
> dom and in stature; is often hungry and weary; meets tempta-
> tion not as God, but as man, "being tempted in all points like
> as we are, yet without sin;" learns obedience "by the things
> which He suffered;" knows not the day of second coming.
> Yet these limitations, self-imposed as they were, do not open
> the way for any dishonoring views regarding His trustworthi-
> ness as a teacher; they do not make of Him the fallible Jewish
> rabbi of modernism. Such inferences from the kenosis are
> hasty and superficial.[17]

16. Morgan, p. 77.
17. McClain, p. 508.

He fulfilled the divine pattern and ideal of human nature, for He did not lower Himself to the level of participation in the sins of degraded humanity but as man was perfect.[18]

It is important to note that the act of incarnation as designated by the expression "was made" (KJV; lit., the Greek aorist participle *genomenos*) was a definite historical event in the course of time. In other words, this was no heavenly apparition or hallucination. Christ *did become* man. He *did enter* into this world as man. This is the definite fact, and it stands in contrast to the eternal preexistence of Christ in the form of God and the continuation of the condition indicated by the expressions "being" (in form of God) and "to be" (equal with God) in verse 6. The contrast is important and involves both time element and essential condition.

The clause "having become in likeness of men" does not mean that the Son ceased to be God, but that the Son of God came to possess true human characteristics in addition to His divine characteristics, which still remained as before. In His preexistent form, in that state of equality with God, the unincarnate Son enjoyed only one mode of consciousness—He could think and feel only as God. But the incarnate Son can think and feel like God and like man. Thus, in the act of self-abasement, of entering into human form and nature, God did not change Himself into a man, but He united Himself with human nature. He assumed the human perspective in a mysterious and glorious way.

18. McClain's comment is noteworthy: "The two phrases *made in likeness of men,* and *being found in fashion as man,* might seem to suggest an unreal, docetic view of Christ's humanity if we were dependent upon these alone for our doctrine of the Incarnation. But we have the whole testimony of the Gospel records to guide us in the interpretation of these expressions, and this testimony affirms that the humanity of our Lord was real. The Apostle's reason for speaking as he does in this text is not to insinuate that Christ was not true man, but probably to remind his readers that there is after all a difference between the man Jesus and man who is a sinner. Sinfulness is not a necessary characteristic of humanity, though it happens to be a universal characteristic of the humanity that we know. Because this last is so, men are in the habit of regarding sinfulness and humanity as correlative terms. Paul's use of "likeness" and "fashion" is the guarded language of inspiration upon a theme where a misstep may invite confusion" (McClain, p. 507).

The Holy Spirit has very carefully chosen the word "likeness" (Gr., *homoiōmati*) to characterize the Lord's human form. It refers to resemblance, representation, that which comes very near to equality or identity but is not quite the same. It is used in Romans 6:5, "planted together in the *likeness* of his death," and in Romans 8:3, "God sending his own Son in the *likeness* of sinful flesh" (italics added). These are good illustrations of the use and meaning of the word. The Lord's humanity was true, a real likeness, no sham; as Wuest remarks, "Not a phantom, nor an incomplete copy of humanity."[19] Christ's humanity was real, as real as ours, but completely apart from the sinfulness of other men. For this reason, the Holy Spirit has used this particular word (*homoiōmati*) for "likeness," its very presence in the sentence providing a safeguard against error.

The likeness was genuine, but the word does not express *all* that Christ was and is. It does not set forth the *whole* of His being. He is neither a divine man nor a human god—but true God and true man, two diverse natures in the one person—God manifest in flesh. This is the distinctive characteristic of the incarnation, and must always remain so in our thinking.[20] The plural form "men" is used in the generic sense, because Christ took the nature of universal humanity, representing not the individual man, but the entire human race.

The sovereign, almighty power of Christ could easily have sustained His body. And though He ate, drank, grew weary, and slept, it might have been only for the eyes of those around Him. But this would not have been man's real, bodily life. Soul, spirit, and body are so wonderfully related and con-

---

19. Kenneth S. Wuest, *Philippians in the Greek New Testament,* p. 68.
20. See H. A. A. Kennedy, "The Epistle to the Philippians," in *The Expositor's Greek Testament,* which states: "Christ's assumption of the form of a slave does not imply that the innermost basis of His personality, His ego, was changed, although indeed there was more in this emptying of Himself than we can think or say. He was true God, and real man" (p. 437).

nected that it would not have been man's life at all. And if the Son of God had not taken for Himself the life of man, no son of man could have received the life God gives to all who believe in His Son. Every true Christian knows what the highest life of all is in fact. Salvation in Christ, trust in God's love, hope in His eternal mercy and grace, that spirit of filial love which submits itself cheerfully and willingly to the will of our heavenly Father—all these give us enablement and strength to serve the Lord, to worship Him, and stand true to Him in this world.

And Christ is the source and fountainhead of this life. But He is something more; He is its great, supreme Example. Possessed of infinite power, He "emptied Himself," looking to the Father constantly for His strength. Possessed of infinite wisdom, He ever lifted up His eyes to heaven for counsel with the Father who abides there. Willing only what was right and good, having no desire but what was pure and true, He nevertheless submitted that will to the Father in all things and continued in never failing fellowship with Him. This took Him to the cross, but it was indeed His course. It was the eternal plan.

A final answer cannot be given to the question that is certain to be asked: How can there be united in one person, perfect and complete deity on the one hand, and perfect and complete humanity on the other? This is the realm where faith must be operative. By faith we know that with God nothing is impossible. We know that the testimony of the Holy Scriptures proves conclusively the union of the two natures in Christ. We know that the one does not contradict the other, and that throughout the life of Christ, there were constant manifestations of the two natures, side by side, the essentials of deity and the facts of humanity. We know that Christ, by His incarnation and subsequent exaltation, amazing as it is, took His human form and nature with Him into heaven, back into the depths of the Godhead, when He ascended.

> No Paean there, no Bacchic song they raise;
> But the three persons of the Trinity,
> And the two natures joined in One they praise.
>
> DANTE

We ponder, and marvel, and lift up our eyes to the Lord above in awe and wonder. The virgin birth and incarnation, the entrance of the Son of God into human life so that He was—and is—true God and true man, is the inexplicable but incontrovertible mystery of godliness.

He is the Word made flesh. He is the Word made flesh in order that men might see and know the true God, so that the world might have an everlasting revelation of the invisible God in bodily form. Thus the innate curiosity and desire to see God could be satisfied. The psalmist said, "My soul thirsteth for God, for the living God" (Psalm 42:2). Philip said to Christ, "Shew us the Father, and it sufficeth us" (John 14:8).

He is the Word made flesh in order that the world might know what life in its essential perfection truly is. Man has never reached God's ideal for a redeemed society, and never will reach it in this present age. That ideal is revealed in the incarnate Lord Jesus Christ and the life that He lived. It can be reached only by knowing Him personally. When He comes, we shall see Him as He is and be like Him, and the ideal humanity will be realized (1 John 3:2). The great passage in 1 Corinthians 15:45-54 is the pledge of what that ideal will be, of what the life of perfection really is, and assures us as to what we shall be.

He is the Word made flesh in order to die for sinners and to share His own eternal life with men. This is the great purpose of the incarnation, for without it there is no atoning death on the cross and no eternal life for mankind. So the

Son of God came into the world "to give his life a ransom for many" (Matt 20:28). He became incarnate in human form so that men "might have life, and . . . have it more abundantly" (John 10:10).

He is the Word made flesh in order that He might be a merciful and faithful High Priest toward God and for us, His believing people. Even the Lord God Almighty must enter into human life in order that He might know it by experience, by living it Himself. So we have a Saviour and God who has first met, endured, suffered, experienced, and overcome the pain, trials, testings, and troubles of this world, of this life in the flesh. Thus, He knows our case, He understands our pains and problems. He can really be touched with the feeling of our infirmities. He is sympathetic, concerned; in all our afflictions He is afflicted. Hence, "in that he himself hath suffered being tempted [tested], he is able to succour them that are tempted" (Heb 2:18). How blessed to know that He has not left us to struggle along down here in the blood and dust and agony of human life, but holds us up in His everlasting embrace. Our hearts cannot help but be moved with love for Him who was willing to come down into the world and live our life before us, and bear our burdens.

These are the great values of the incarnation. It is, in itself, an impenetrable mystery. We meditate in the sacred Word, and exhaust the limits of our poor minds, without having arrived at the place of final answer. But let us remember that Christ emptied Himself, enduring infinite self-abasement for our salvation and for our everlasting blessedness. He looked not upon His own things except to decide that He would not selfishly grasp the prize of equality with God to Himself at the expense of the redemption of men. He looked beyond to the things of others, *and He put us before Himself, above Himself.* This was His mind. And, in the words of Dr. McClain:

We must at last fall down upon our knees before the mystery of God in Christ and confess humbly that we cannot explain Him. But thank God that we know Him![21]

21. From Alva J. McClain's lectures in Systematic Theology, Grace Theological Seminary, Winona Lake, Ind., 1943.

4

THE CRUCIFIXION OF CHRIST

And being found in fashion as a man, he humbled himself, and became obedient unto death, even the death of the cross (Phil 2:8).

The incarnation was the means by which our Lord bound Himself to our degraded, woeful circumstances of life and carried to us the gracious benefits with which He would enrich us. He came to earth, lived the life of a man, taught and healed, called His twelve, knowing all the while that a shameful and painful death awaited Him. But His death was for our sins, endured by Him in order that we might live with Him in eternity.

Death is often considered the signature of failure and disgrace. When people die, their endeavor and usefulness are past, done; their worth is measured and exhausted; they die, and all is over. The Scriptures teach us that death entered by sin, and eternal separation from God in the place of the lost dead is the end of all who do not know the Saviour, Jesus Christ our Lord.

But the cruel and violent death of crucifixion, inflicted for the worst crimes, is the most disgraceful of all. What it meant for the Lord we cannot begin to measure. We know that He looked ahead to it with the most solemn expectation and that His soul was troubled at the prospect (John 12:24-27). When it came He submitted to the awful degradation, subjected to the blight of death by which He made atonement and finished the transgression. But in this passage the apostle Paul does not dwell on the reasons why the Lord's obedience had to take this road. It is enough when he declares that for our welfare and the glorious achievement of the Father's purpose, Christ lowered Himself to so great a depth and became obedient to the death of a cross. Our Lord said to John: "I am the One living and was dead" (Rev 1:18, author's trans.). The self-emptying and the humiliating obedience to death on the cross was complete.

THE CONDITION OF CHRIST AS BEHELD BY MEN

Despite differences of opinion with regard to the punctuation in this paragraph, the reading of the King James Version and the American Standard Version of 1901 gives to the passage a harmonious and majestic movement and places upon each clause its proper emphasis. The paragraph is a graphic description of the preincarnate Son, His descent into humanity, His condition as true man among men, and the extended humbling to the lowest point—the awful death of one accursed on a cross. And all of this was for the redemption of lost sinners like ourselves.

In the phrase "And being found in fashion as a man," the verbal expression "being found" (*heuretheis*) is the aorist passive participle of the verb *heuriskō*, "find by inquiry, thought, examination, scrutiny, observation, and hearing; to see, learn, understand by discovery." Here it has the sense of "being discovered, recognized; one's character and state as found out by others."[1] This verb in the aorist tense points back to the time of the Lord's life on earth when He lived as a man in the world of men.

The word rendered "fashion" (*schēma*) is important to our understanding of this statement. It describes the externals of human nature, that which is purely outward and which ap-

1. See also Luke 17:18; 2 Corinthians 11:12; Revelation 5:4.

peals to the senses, such as countenance, figure, bearing, speech, actions, and manner of life.[2] "Form" (*morphēn*) denotes that which is intrinsic and essential, while "likeness" (*homoiōmati*) states the fact of real similarity. "Fashion" (*schēmati*) is not interested in probing the inner reality, but denotes the outward appearance of something.

The statement is that Christ was "found in fashion *as a man.*" The words "as a man" maintain the idea of *likeness* pointed out in verse 7, and continue the remarkable choice of words with which the apostle, under the control of the Holy Spirit, guards the idea of Christ's person. As regards fashion, mode, and habit, our Lord Jesus Christ, truly man, was found by other men to be so. His appearance, dress, bearing, and language all gave the impression of real humanity. In every aspect of appearance, He made Himself known as man. His growth from infancy to adulthood followed the course of all other men, apart from the presence of sin. The full record is set forth in the gospels and attested in Acts and the epistles. Bring the eyewitnesses together and put the question to them: Was Jesus Christ a real man? They respond with a unanimous yes. In Christ they saw one like themselves.[3]

Our Lord was found in fashion as a man, in all outward respects like other men. Can words express more strongly how wonderful it is in the apostle's mind that the Lord should be so found? But being so, He humbled Himself to a strange and remarkable obedience. Subjection, and in that subjection *obedience,* is the part of every creature. But the obedi-

2. See also its use in 1 Corinthians 7:31.
3. In view of the current overstress by so many upon the *humanity* of Christ, and the consequent lack of proper emphasis upon His deity and sovereign lordship, it should be reiterated that Christ was not merely man and nothing else—not only man, but the eternal Son of God manifest in the flesh, form, and nature of man; there was no observed difference between His appearance and that of any other man. To the argument of those who stress the humanity of Christ above His deity, we answer: Yes! He was, and is, perfect man, but He is so much more than man that the expressions "in likeness of men" and "as a man" must have justified themselves to the believing minds of Paul's readers without any misconception.

ence which Christ was required to learn was most particular and unusual. A heavy burden was laid upon the Lord. He was made under the Law; and bearing the burden of all human sin, He wrought redemption for the race. In all outward respects, our Lord was like other men. Yet He had a mission unlike all other men, and the fact that He was *not merely a man* is conveyed by the expression "in fashion as a man." Gough-Pidge says:

> Before (v. 6), Paul used the strongest language concerning Christ's pre-existence, "Who, being in form of God," here, and in v. 7, with an evident feeling of the peculiar character of Christ's humanity, a humanity wholly unique, he says: "being made in *the likeness* of men," and "being found in fashion as a man."[4]

The Course of Lowly Obedience Chosen by Christ

The One who was found in fashion as a man "humbled himself, and became obedient unto death." This is the path of voluntary obedience from the humble birth to the grave, the lowly path that Christ chose for Himself. He persevered in, and carried out, the purpose for which He became man. Having become man in order that He might be a bondslave, a servant of God and of men, He then gave Himself up to the service for which He came down from heaven; He became obedient. This submission deepened into the experience of death—obedience carried to its limit. We must not err in thinking that the obedience of Christ was like that of a yoked field horse. Our Lord gave the Father perfect obedience, but He Himself was involved in the planning, and His obedience was born out of voluntary choice to suffer the agony of crucifixion in our behalf.

When we come to these words we are brought to a stop, and must bow our heads in silent meditation and wondering

4. J. B. Gough-Pidge, *The Epistle to the Philippians,* in *An American Commentary on the New Testament,* 5:30.

awe at what we read. We find that we cannot restrain the tears of sorrow and heartfelt gratitude, as the Holy Spirit constrains us with these words.

"He humbled himself" sets forth the Lord's extended humiliation. The verb "humbled" retains the old idea of "abase," and is the same word which Paul uses in verse 3 when he exhorts believers to exercise "lowliness of mind" in their attitude toward each other. The New Testament ennobles the term, but the basic idea of "bring low, abase" remains. The ennobling of the word is to be found in the sense to which it is put by inspiration, in connection with Christ's voluntary course of humble obedience for the redemption of men. It is impossible to read this statement and not be stirred by it.

The verb "humbled" is in the aorist tense, and the apostle uses the active voice with the reflexive pronoun "himself," which intensifies the thought. Here, plainly stated, is the *fact* of the Lord's humbling. Christ lowered, humbled His own person. All was voluntary, prompted by His infinite love *for us*. This is what must have been in Paul's mind when he wrote to the Galatians: "Christ . . . loved me, and gave himself for me" (Gal 2:20). It is the greatest moral dynamic laid down anywhere for men, and it is found again here: "He humbled himself." McClain calls attention to this expression of self-humbling:

> An impressive thought in both of the steps in Christ's humiliation is the perfect *freedom* and *voluntariness* of the Son of God. No theory of the kenosis can be true which brings Him into an earthly state where it is impossible for Him to assert "equality with God." Room must be left for a voluntary perseverance not to assert that equality, on the part of the One who could do otherwise. He assumed servanthood and died on the cross for us, not because of any compulsion external to Himself, but according to the free and loving choice of His own will. He was no Victim of a secret and irresistible destiny such as that which, in the Stoic's theology,

swept the gods of Olympus to their hour of change and ex-
tinction as surely as it swept men to their ultimate annihila-
tion. When He stooped to servanthood and death, He did so
with all the sovereign free will of One whose choices are
limited only by His own holy and loving will. He *emptied
Himself.* He *humbled Himself.*[5]

As One obedient, Christ gave Himself up wholly to the
Father's will. His obedience is described by a most significant
Greek word, *hupēkoos,* derived from a verb which literally
means "hear under." This is both descriptive and appropriate.
The preposition "under" depicts the Lord's humble state of
slavehood, and the verb "hear" denotes His obedient atten-
tiveness to the Father's will.

The picture in this word is beautifully portrayed in Isaiah
50:4, in the prophet's description of the Saviour: "The Lord
GOD hath given me the tongue of the learned, that I should
know how to speak a word in season to him that is weary: he
wakeneth morning by morning, he wakeneth mine ear to hear
as . . . [they that are taught]." The image is of a master wak-
ening his pupils early for instruction. The inspired writer
uses it to depict the humiliation of Christ. He was prepared
to receive the instruction of the Father, to be taught by Him,
to learn obedience, "not rebellious, neither turned away back"
(Isa 50:5). He is shown as ready to do the Father's will in
procuring salvation for men at the cost of His own obedient
suffering. Isaiah's portrayal is reproduced in Hebrews 5:8-9.

The obedience led Him to death, and to death in its most
degrading form. It is difficult, in fact impossible, for us to
realize what a tremendous descent our Lord's humiliation
was. If we as intelligent beings were to undergo some extraordinary change, and be lowered to incarnation in the lowest
creature that crawls upon the earth, it would not be so great
a descent for us as it was for the Son of God to become incar-

5. Ibid.

nate, and then go on to the further descent into death. Christ
not only lived human life, He also died human death. Caffin
says, "What a step downward this was! We may be feeble
and dependent, still we are alive. And how great is the difference between the living and the dead! The One who but
yesterday had taught and cheered, and comforted and blessed
His Apostles, now lay before them, dead. A second step in
Christ's descent indeed! From the throne of God to the grave
of man!"[6]

The word "unto" is to be taken in the sense of *extent*, so
that Christ is dramatically described going to the very extremity of obedience. The descent of Christ is intensified by
that modest word. The mind of our Lord is revealed here in
a most significant way. As McClain points out:

> This voluntary perseverance in that mind which led Him
> first to the kenosis and finally to the cross has an important
> bearing on the problem of His self-consciousness. It implies
> a certain continuity of self-consciousness throughout all the
> changes incident to His earthly state. He knew, while on
> earth, of His pre-existent state; He was aware of the mind
> which had actuated Him in exchanging the God-form for
> the servant-form; and He purposed to have "that mind in
> Him" down to the last act in the great drama of redemption.
> "I know whence I came and whither I go," He said to the
> Pharisees. And drawing near to the hour of death, He re-
> pelled all suggestions of any possible change in His own eter-
> nal purpose by declaring steadily: "But for this cause came
> I unto this hour" (Jn. 8:14; 12:27). But the writer of the
> Philippian letter will not permit us to forget that, even while
> our blessed Lord was acting in the manner of a sovereign, He
> was also acting in filial obedience to the Father's will. In
> humbling Himself, He became "obedient" unto death—not
> that He was obeying death when He died, but in dying He
> was obeying the Father whose bondservant He had come to

6. B. C. Caffin, *Philippians*, in *The Pulpit Commentary*, 47:79.

be. The thought is that He obeyed God so utterly as to die.[7]

He did not shrink even from death and the awful suffering and torture that accompanied it. He need not have gone to this extremity, because He was without sin, the perfect man, the Son of God; and because of this, greater was His suffering. With deliberate consideration, with full knowledge of all it would mean for Him, our Lord yielded Himself willingly to death. He had the power to lay down His life—no man could take it from Him—and He exercised that power freely. Although He was the Lord of glory, with dominion over all, yet "we see Jesus, who was made a little lower than the angels for the suffering of death" (Heb 2:9*a*). Thus, we behold the final step.

THE CLIMAX IN THE DEATH OF CHRIST ON A CROSS

The final words of this great paragraph, "death of the cross," must cause us the deepest humility. We must stop, linger, and meditate over these words. It was no common, ordinary death. There was mystery in it. How the eternal Son of God, One with the Father in the Godhead, could be abandoned and forsaken by the Father is beyond our capacity of understanding. This much we know with certainty: Christ the Son humbled Himself to the death of a cross; He took our place and bore our sins, He died our death and entered into our doom. Hence, He had to go out into the darkness alone, forsaken by God, to suffer spiritual death: "My God, my God, why hast thou forsaken me?" (Psalm 22:1; Matt 27:46).

Then physical death came almost at once. Matthew 27:45-50 and John 19:30-34 demonstrate the certainty of His death. It was a shameful death, involving not only intense suffering but extreme degradation as well. It was torture that led to death, and that in full public view. While the body hung helpless, the victim's emotions and self-image were on the

7. McClain, p. 509.

cross too. He could not hide from the curious; He could not conceal His shame. He could not hope for reprieve or mercy. It was the mode of punishment reserved by the Romans for criminals and slaves.

The final word, "cross" (Gr., *stauros*), shows the full significance of the death. Among the Jews it was regarded as entailing a curse, for the Mosaic Law had so pronounced. It was the death of one *accursed, accursed of God*. The great declaration of this is Galatians 3:13: "Christ hath redeemed us from the curse of the law, being made a curse for us: for it is written, Cursed is every one that hangeth on a tree." The "tree" here is the cross of Christ.

In accomplishing our release from the Law's curse and from sin's bondage, the Lord was "made a curse for us." He was not turned into the form and character of a curse, but the Law which demanded that guilty sinners die satisfied its demands on Him, and thus thrust Him out of the pale of legal jurisdiction. God's wrath descended upon Him, not because our curse had affected Him through contact with us but because He bore our whole curse upon Himself. We were under the curse, and Christ took that curse upon Himself and away from us by placing Himself over us, so that when divine judgment fell, it fell upon Him instead of us (Matt 20:28; 1 Tim 2:6; 1 Pet 3:18).

A thoughtful reader imbued with the temper of our times might ask, Is it not within the power of God to forgive without seeking retribution? We must always bear in mind that God's justice does not follow the lines of man's justice. Sin is never ignored or glossed over. The sinner is always accountable. Sin deserves retribution just as surely as righteousness deserves reward. God would have acted in flat contradiction to His nature had He glossed over the guilt of mankind. He would have denied Himself if He had uttered the pardon before payment was tendered.

Therefore, let us not fashion our faith according to the variable winds of human justice. We are dealing with no arbitrary human court here. The sovereign, holy God turned His face from His Son as sin and guilt plunged upon the Lord hanging on the cross. The righteous rule of God prevailed, and the atoning sacrifice was done.

Through centuries of difficulty and debate, the true church has held tenaciously to the substitutionary atonement of Jesus Christ. He bore the weight and penalty of sin in our place. On our behalf He took the thunderbolt of God's wrath. For the sake of sinners He died the death of one accursed.

The great and blessed proclamation of the gospel is that Christ has purchased men's freedom from the curse of the Law, which demands death. Here is the great historical *fact* of redemption. The aorist verb in Galatians 3:13, "redeemed" (Gr., *exegorasen*), points out a purchasing once for all by the payment of a ransom price, by which a man is bought out of the slave market. Christ was *Himself* the price laid down in death.

When we behold the cross, we cannot think of noble martyrdom, but our minds are filled with the realization that the awful curse did not fall—cannot ever fall—upon us, because Christ was there in our place to bear it for us. Such was the great purpose of the incarnation, and such was the exhibition of the mind of Christ. He went through infinite self-abasement for our salvation. He looked not merely to His own things, but beyond to the things of others. He put *us* before Himself. He did not cling to His divine position and glory as that which would enrich Him, that never could be parted with by Him, but He emptied Himself that He might grasp us eternally in His saving love. This led Him inevitably to the death of a cross. He became our Substitute. Lenski's splendid comment is:

> Here is the climax of it all, leaving all unsanctified reasoning utterly behind. He who was the Son of God, He who communicated His divine attributes to His human nature, so that

all the Godhead dwelt in Him bodily (Col. 2:9), *He died,* died hanging on a post of wood, the mark of being accursed. Of His own volition, hence the most noble act the world has ever seen, hence full of infinite merit, all this to be bestowed upon us. This is the mystery of the Gospel, into which even the angels of God delight to look. This is the historic Gospel fact, which the Gospel attests and publishes in all the world. This is the fact that saves to the uttermost all those who embrace it in confidence and trust, and rest their very soul upon it.[8]

Hence, the incarnation provided for the salvation of sinners, for the reconciliation of mankind lost and without hope. "To wit, that God was in Christ, reconciling the world unto himself, not imputing their trespasses unto them" (2 Cor 5: 19). "Yet now hath he reconciled *in the body of his flesh* through death" (Col 1:21-22, italics added). In short, the incarnation prepared for the atonement: "Christ Jesus came into the world to save sinners" (1 Tim 1:15; cf. 1 John 3:5), by His sacrificial death on a cross at Calvary.

The Unitarian-liberal view that the death of Christ was merely exemplary contradicts the teaching of the Scriptures. It necessitates a surrender of the other great doctrines of the Christian faith. If the Lord was simply a martyr, even a great and good man, the "noblest flower of humanity," He could not possibly be a perfect example. The influence of Christ's example has no power to lead sinners to a life of holiness. The daily life of godliness comes only after atoning sacrifice has been made for our sins.

The great passages in the Word of God which set forth our Lord Jesus Christ as the supreme Example, at the same time show Him to be the "propitiation for our sins" (1 John 2:2). The passage in Philippians 2:5-11 is the outstanding example. Christ did nothing merely for the sake of example; even His baptism was a symbol of His sacrificial death on the cross.

8. Lenski, p. 791.

The great number of scriptural references to the death of Christ as the source of our salvation, as well as the symbolism in the ordinances, cannot be explained by a theoretical view of the Lord as a mere example. The atoning death of Christ is the central theme of the Holy Scriptures and the basic truth of Christianity. It was not simply the final incident in His career, but the real ground for forgiveness of sins and admission to heaven.

Other modern liberal theologians insist that the death of Christ was nothing more than the tragic fate of a notable and intelligent man who died for a cause which He mistakenly espoused. Bultmann has carried this idea even further when he says that Christ suffered the death of a political criminal on the cross because His ministry was "misunderstood as something political." His life and experience, and His sufferings which climaxed in His death were in vain. We really do not and cannot know exactly how the Lord understood His death. Such a radical misinterpretation of Christ's death is frightening. For if the Lord's death has no redemptive significance, there is no message for us to proclaim to the world. What these modern critics are saying is, in essence, that Christ died without cause, becoming a martyr for a mistaken ideal, for a mission destined for ignominious defeat.

But the cross was *not* a defeat. The sufferings of Christ were borne *in the stead of sinners,* and were thus both propitiatory and penal—necessary, not simply to reveal the love of God, but also to satisfy His justice. Our blessed Lord had to die to save us from our sins and to share with us His own eternal life. "And as Moses lifted up the serpent in the wilderness, even so must the Son of man be lifted up: that whosoever believeth in him should not perish, but have eternal life" (John 3:14-15).

Amid all the evidence that the death of Christ was a lasting victory, there is perhaps no single point more significant than the simple action of the soldiers described in John 19:2:

"The soldiers platted a *crown of thorns,* and put it on his head" (italics added). The word "crown" is the Greek *stephanos,* a term which denoted royalty or exalted rank. It was used to describe the garland given as the prize to victors in the Greek games. It signified military valor, civic worth, nuptial joy, festal gladness, regality, victory in the public games. It is in particular the crown of victory, the insignia of triumph. The mocking soldiers dressed the Lord as a king and improvised a crown for Him in the presence of Pilate, who directed the scourging and derision. It was a crown of thorny twigs wound together and pressed down upon Christ's head. It served a double purpose: to make Christ ridiculous, and to make Him suffer further. Trickles of blood disfigured the Lord's face—not with the artistic elegance which many modern painters have portrayed, but with the awfulness of cruel reality. His sufferings were extreme and very real, as was necessary for His bearing of human sin and sorrow. The crown was a striking symbol of the consequences of the Fall being laid upon the head of our great Substitute.[9]

Yet, despite this mockery, the crown of thorns bespeaks something further. With all its indescribable brutality, the

9. Bruce writes most fittingly: "Not that the sufferings of Christ are to be treated as of no moment. By no means: it was worthy of God to make His appointed Captain of salvation perfect through suffering. It was a signal proof both of His love and of His wisdom. Of His love, because in Christ now exalted to heavenly glory, and having the keys of kingdom of heaven in His hands, but once a suffering man like ourselves, He hath given us a Saviour who, having fully experienced all the evils to which we are liable, is able to sympathize with us and willing to succour us. Of His wisdom, because the curriculum of suffering through which He appointed the Saviour to pass was congruous to the vocation of the latter. It is fit that a captain should have full experience of military hardships: no one can be a good captain on any other terms. How can he lead an army to victory and glory, who shirks the risks of battle and the privations of the campaign? Therefore He is a good Captain, having descended personally into the scene of strife and become Himself a combatant, and stood in the very forefront of the battle, He draws us on to glory, honour, and immortality by the inspiration of His example. Looking unto Jesus the Author and Finisher of faith, who for the joy that was set before Him endured the cross, despising the shame and is set down at the right hand of the throne of God, we resist unto blood, striving against sin, and so pass on into the eternal kingdom" (A. B. Bruce, *The Humiliation of Christ* [Grand Rapids: Eerdmans, 1955], p. 297. Used by permission).

crown was not only a wreath of pain and humiliation. It was also a mark of victory. For although the Lord of glory must first die, He could not be held in the grasp of death. As He passed on through the death, He came into a new life in the resurrection and return to glory. He had, through deep sorrow and suffering, wrought eternal redemption for sinners— a redemption which meets all difficulties and which opens heaven to all believers. He was—and is—the great Victor, having gained victory over every form and force of evil and over death itself. The symbolism of the crown is fittingly summarized by Paul in Colossians 2:13-15. Unknowingly, the soldiers pressed the crown of thorns upon the head of Him who is indeed King of kings and Lord of lords.

If we were to study in detail the redemptive work of our blessed Lord, it would become clear that the experience of the Son of God consisted in a series of triumphs. From His determination not to grasp selfishly the powers of deity and sovereignty, all the way through to His exaltation, there is the blessedness of victory. So all those who have trusted in Christ for salvation may stand with Him, and say with holy fear, yet with conviction, "Therefore my heart is glad, and my glory rejoiceth: my flesh also shall rest in hope" (Psalm 16:9; cf. Acts 2:26). "Death is swallowed up in victory. Thanks be to God, which giveth us the victory through our Lord Jesus Christ" (1 Cor 15:54, 57).

By the grace of God, let us lay deeply to heart the great facts of Philippians 2:5-11. In Christ is the revelation of God's purpose for every true Christian: a mind motivated by truth and love, and a life submitted to the Lord. It must be a life of self-emptying service and suffering for Him and of sacrificial regard for the things of others. How distinctly vainglory, glorying in *empty things,* is exposed in the wondrous light of the Lord's *self-emptying.* The greatest injunction laid upon Christians in the New Testament is this: "Let this mind be in you, which was also in Christ Jesus."

Oh, to be but emptier, lowlier,
Mean, unnoticed, and unknown,
And to God a vessel holier,
Filled with Christ, and Christ alone!

TRANS. FRANCES BEVAN

5

THE EXALTATION OF CHRIST

Wherefore God also hath highly exalted him, and given him a name which is above every name: that at the name of Jesus every knee should bow, . . . and that every tongue should confess that Jesus Christ is Lord, to the glory of God the Father (Phil 2:9-11).

Verses 9 through 11 of Philippians 2 form the grand climax of the whole passage. The great basis upon which the practical admonition of verses 1 through 5 rests is the Lord's humiliation and exaltation; Christ humbled Himself, "wherefore . . . God . . . highly exalted him." Exaltation follows self-abasement, glory follows humility. Christ became obedient unto death, and God gave to Him "a name which is above every name." Unto Jesus Christ, the God-man, all power is given in heaven and on earth, all the unutterable glory and majesty of the Godhead. But it was the human nature of our Lord that experienced the exaltation, just as it underwent the humiliation. Because of this, whereas Christ humbled and lowered *Himself, God* exalted Him.

In Christ was fulfilled the divine principle He had given to His followers: "And whosoever shall exalt himself shall be abased; and he that shall humble himself shall be exalted" (Matt 23:12; Luke 14:11; 18:14). Our Lord continually taught this simple truth. "Except a man be born again" (John 3:3); "Blessed are the poor in spirit" (Matt 5:3); "He that humbleth himself" (Luke 14:11). He Himself is the great example of His own teaching. He humbled Himself as no other could ever humble himself. He is exalted as no other can be exalted.

We can be exalted only as He was—through genuine humility. We, as our Lord, must humble ourselves *in the path of obedience and resolve to do God's will.* The Lord humbled Himself, but He did not then seek glory and enrichment as His "due." God exalted Him at the proper time. In the light of Christ's humility and exaltation, no true Christian seeks to exalt himself. The highest glory never comes to those who seek it for themselves. It is always conferred upon those who are truly humble and self-forgetful. If we are wise, we shall gladly and willingly humble ourselves in the assurance that self-abasement is the plain and only path of real exaltation. Let us not complain in our state of humbleness.

THE RAISING OF CHRIST TO UNIVERSAL DIGNITY AND POWER

With respect to the raising of Christ, two items are to be noted in verse 9: (1) the nature of the exaltation of Christ, and (2) the name conferred upon Christ.

THE NATURE OF THE EXALTATION OF CHRIST

The first sentence in verse 9 reads: "Wherefore God also hath highly exalted him." The writer to the Hebrews testifies in a similar fashion: "But we see Jesus, who was made a little lower than the angels for the suffering of death, crowned with glory and honour" (Heb 2:9). God gave this special approbation to the Son because of the Son's obedience and the perfection of His service, climaxed by the awful death on a cross, but especially because of the mind of Christ revealed in His self-forgetting devotion and determination. *Therefore* God highly exalted Him.

Christ is the absolute revelation of the Father. All through His life, the Father's heart as well as the Son's was disclosed. Christ's heart was always in fellowship with the Father's; the two were always one. The Father's heart delighted in the Son, and the Son always did the will of the Father. The Son was sent forth into the world to become one of us and to live before us, and He finished His course. It was fitting for the Father to approve and to crown the Son's service. The Son, who so esteemed His great mission in the world and who did the will of His Father in giving Himself for us, could take His place of exaltation because of His obedience and His *mind.*

Let us note carefully that at the heart of His majesty and dignity, His sovereignty and eternity, the greatness of His condescension, His perfection of obedience and endurance, His patience and long-suffering, and His final indescribable courage, was *the mind of the Lord,* upon which the Father fixed His vision and which should be the object of ours. The plan established by Father, Son, and Holy Spirit in timeless ages was executed at immense personal cost. The holy Trinity was at work: the Father enabling, the Son obeying, the Spirit mediating. Redemption was accomplished, the work completed. Christ's mind was intent on the glory of God and the salvation of men. Never laying aside or emptying Himself of anything due to the Father, or of all that befits and belongs to Him as God the Son, His heart went out to mankind and His course shaped itself to the needs of men as He looked upon the fallen race. This was the mind of the Good Shepherd, who laid down His life for the sheep. This was what consecrated and completed His service and received the Father's triumphant approbation.

How all this was and is in the eternal Son of God and the plan of God, we cannot possibly conceive. But we own it all to be there. We bow before the revelation of the mind of Christ, and marvel at it, knowing that His way is the right way. "For ye know the grace of our Lord Jesus Christ, that, though he was rich, yet for your sakes he became poor, that ye through his poverty might be rich" (2 Cor 8:9). Wherefore God highly exalted Him.

Have you yielded to this way that is His? Are you willing to renounce the love of this world age, the lusting flesh, and the pride of life, which set you at odds with Christ? Then let this mind be in you which was also in Christ Jesus. *Let it be in you.* "Look not every man on his own things, but every man also on the things of others" (Phil 2:4). "Let nothing be done through strife or vainglory" (Phil 2:3). "Let all bitterness, and wrath, and anger, and clamour [envy], and evil speaking, be put away from you . . . and be ye kind one to another, forgiving one another, even as God for Christ's sake hath forgiven you" (Eph 4:31-32). Recognize that you are here on earth for someone else's furtherance and joy in faith. Let this mind be in you; if it be in you, it will find ways of showing itself. And in humbling yourself, you will be exalted in due time.

The verb in the first statement of verse 9 carries the superlative idea: God *supremely* exalted Him. It is an extraordinary antithesis to the words of the preceding verse, "He humbled himself, and became obedient unto death, even the death of a cross" (v. 8). Our blessed Lord passed from a state of degradation to one of exaltation. There was no change in person, but a change of position, place, condition—from the lowest to the highest. We should rejoice because He is where He is today. The Lord said to His apostles: "If ye loved me, ye would rejoice, because I said, I go unto the Father" (John 14:28). We are not without likeness to our Lord, yet we come short in showing to the world the whole mind of Christ. We often "shew [forth] the Lord's death" (1 Cor 11:26), but in His death were the mighty life and conclusive triumph of His power, grace, and love. Therefore, let us show forth His life as well as His death, for we serve a risen Lord.

In its essence, the exaltation had three aspects:

1. Christ's resumption of the independent use of the divine attributes. These were held in abeyance when Christ em-

tied Himself to take servant form, but now they are once again at the Lord's command.

2. The Saviour's withdrawal of all limitations and restrictions in His communication of divine fullness to His human nature. The fullness of Deity flows through the fullness of perfect humanity.

3. The exercise, on the part of the human nature of Christ, of all the powers that belonged to it by virtue of its union with the divine.[1] Limited in their exercise during Christ's earthly life, those powers are now resident in their full potential.

In its exercise, the exaltation of Christ was historical and included the events of both the resurrection (Luke 24:50-51) and the ascension (Acts 1:10-11), as pointed to by the aorist tense of the verb "exalted" (*huperupsosen*). The verb shows the change in position, but not in person, in the exaltation of Christ. It is formed by the preposition *huper,* meaning "over, above," and *hupsoō,* "lift up high, exalt"; so it means "making high in position, raising up to the highest rank."

The end of the resurrection and ascension was Christ's sitting down at the right hand of God (Col 3:1; Heb 10:12-13). Strong says:

> As the resurrection proclaimed Christ to mankind as the perfected and glorified Man, the conqueror of sin and Lord of death, the Pioneer and consummator of our faith, so the ascension proclaimed Him to the universe as the reinstated Sovereign, the risen Lord, possessor of universal dominion, the omnipresent Object of worship[2]

1. A. H. Strong adds: "The eighth Psalm, with its account of the glory of human nature, is at present fulfilled only in Christ (See Heb. 2:9). Christ's human body was not necessarily subject to death; only by outward compulsion or voluntary surrender could He die. Hence resurrection was a natural necessity (Ac. 2:24, 31). This exaltation, which then affected humanity only in its Head, is to be the experience also of the members" (*Systematic Theology,* p. 706).
2. Ibid., p. 708.

The Son of Man was raised from the dead and He returned to the habitation of God. He has taken His human form and nature back into heaven, and He is there now, our great High Priest, at the right hand of God, glorified in His human nature with the glory He had in His divine nature before the foundation of the world.

This is the great practical importance of the ascension. It means that we have now in heaven a great and wonderful Intercessor and Advocate with God the Father; "wherefore he is able also to save them to the uttermost that come unto God by him, seeing he ever liveth to make intercession for them" (Heb 7:25). And let us remember, "We have not an high priest which cannot be touched with the feeling of our infirmities; but was in all points tempted like as we are, yet without sin" (Heb 4:15).

The exalted Lord Jesus Christ has resumed His glory in the resurrection and ascension, and the seating at the right hand of God, since the purpose for which He assumed a slave's form has been accomplished. But the thought is not at all that only now His human nature has received the "form of God" and the condition of equality, as some insist. The human nature of Christ, by virtue of the one person, partook of these already in the incarnation, when the actual union of the two natures took place. Lenski remarks:

> Now, after the slave's form has been dropped, the human nature has ceased the limited use of its communicated divine attributes required for the work of redeeming us, and entered upon the plenary, unlimited use of these attributes consequent upon redemption in the full royal work of Jesus.[3]

And Strong says:

> So the Acts of the Apostles speak constantly of the Son of Man, of the Man Jesus as God, ever present, the Object of

3. R. C. H. Lenski, *The Interpretation of St. Paul's Epistles to the Galatians, to the Ephesians, and to the Philippians,* p. 794.

worship, seated at the right hand of God, having all the powers and prerogatives of Deity. Then who and what is this Christ who is present with us when we pray? The Christ who is present with His people when they pray is not simply the Logos, or the divine nature of Christ—His humanity being separated from the divinity and being localized in heaven. This would be inconsistent with His promise, "Lo, I am with you alway," in which the "I" that spoke was not simply Deity, but Deity and humanity inseparably united; and it would deny the real and indissoluble union of the two natures.[4]

In its extent, the exaltation is unlimited. The verb indicates the fact that the change of position was a *super change,* a change far beyond the ordinary. The risen Lord has gone into heaven, and He manifests Himself there as our High Priest, the God-man, and Lord over the nations. But He has also gone *far above* all heavens, that He may fill all things (Eph 1:23). Ephesians 1:20-21 describes the infinite power, glory, authority, and majesty which the ascended Lord Jesus Christ exercises completely at God's right hand. In His state of humiliation, Christ exercised these powers only to the extent that they were necessary to His work of redemption, and then always in full accord with the Father's will and purpose. His obedience was absolute. But now, in His present exalted state, He exercises them all in the infinite way.

Both the raising and seating of Christ at the right hand of God pertain to His human nature, as does the "placing of all things under His feet" (Eph 1:22, author's trans.). The full glory of the exaltation is brought out by the descriptive words which set forth the raising of the Lord "far above all principality, and power, and might, and dominion, and every name that is named" (v. 21).

Ephesians 4:10 reveals that the resurrection and ascension exalted Him "far above all heavens, that he might fill all

4. Strong, p. 709.

things." The exaltation of Christ "far above all heavens" does not imply that He occupies some place far beyond all the heavens, beyond where God and the angels are, but that the ascended Lord has sovereignty over all the heavens. To be far above the heavens cannot be some place that is not heaven. Where could such a place as that be? As Lenski remarks:

> He has ascended, not merely as any other saint, but as the Apostle testifies, above all heavens, and also truly fills all things, and being everywhere present, not only as God, but also as Man, rules from sea to sea, and to the ends of the earth.[5]

THE NAME CONFERRED UPON CHRIST

The apostle says, "And given him a name which is above every name." The humiliation of Christ, that is, His coming down from heaven, the emptying and lowering of Himself as man, were not granted to Him, or bestowed upon Him, or provided for Him, but were *voluntarily done* by the Lord Himself. The crowning of all this, however, when the work was finished, was something which God the Father could do, and which He did by definite act, as a gift of infinite love, approval, and grace. He conferred upon the Son "the name which is above every name."[6]

It should be pointed out, before attempting to determine what this name may be, that it is first of all a *transcendant name;* it is above every name. There is no other name like it in the whole universe. It cannot be uttered with neutrality or passivity. It is ideally and independently perfect, and no other name can be compared or likened to it.

Second, it is a name that *requires universal acknowledg-*

5. Lenski, pp. 524-25.
6. The definite article occurs before the noun "name" in the first instance. It is *"The* name" (*to onoma*), not "a name" as the KJV renders. The article identifies and particularizes the noun, and helps us to establish what "the name" is.

ment and worship. Every knee must bow in homage, obeisance, and confession to the Son. Unsurpassed force and energy are in this name. It has wrought wonders in the earth
and in the minds and hearts of men. It gains the mastery
over the soul, and sends humans to their knees at its knowledge and utterance. It takes the ascendancy over all the
minds in the universe, those in heaven, in the earth, and under
the earth.

Third, this name is *sovereign and awe-inspiring.* It is the
name which corresponds to the Lord's position. It marks the
station and sphere of honor, dignity, and glory of Him who
bears the name. The name is descriptive of the One to whom
it is given, before whom all must fall upon their faces.

Fourth, it is a *God-glorifying name.* Every tongue will confess that Jesus Christ is Lord "to the glory of God the Father"
(Phil 2:11*b*). Acknowledgment of the glory of Christ is acknowledgment of the glory of the Father as the source of
deity and authority manifested perfectly in the Son. It seems
apparent that the name must be *Lord* (Gr., *Kurios*), or as in
the Old Testament, *Jehovah.* The first is the New Testament
equivalent of the second.

Opinion is nevertheless divided as to the identity of this
name. Some commentators argue that it refers to the supreme dignity and honor of the Son in His exalted position.
There is no doubt that His present position of exaltation is
one of the greatest honor, dignity, and majesty; but that these
characteristics equal His name is doubtful.

Others say the name is *Jesus,* His personal, human name,
which means "Jehovah is salvation." But this name was given
to Him at His virgin birth, the token of His humiliation and
His redemptive mission, and was not the name that God conferred upon Him when He exalted Him.

Others insist that the name is *Christ,* which means
"Anointed One." But this was not properly a name. It was

a title, an official designation, drawn from the Jewish usage of anointing, and taken from the verb *chriō*, "to anoint in a sacred manner." After His baptism and the coming of the Holy Spirit upon Him to set Him apart for His great work, He became known by His disciples as "the Anointed One, Messiah." Only gradually, and some time later, did this become a proper name, and it was commonly united with the personal name *Jesus* to form the compound *Jesus Christ*, which, still later, became prevalent in the church.

Still others hold to the name, or title, *Son of God*. Christ continually spoke of God as His Father, implying the relation of a unique sonship. No one will deny that the relation between Father and Son in the Godhead was unique and incomprehensible. He responded to this name ("the Christ, the Son of the living God"), although His favorite designation of Himself, or at least the one He used of Himself more often than any other, was *Son of man*. Still, the name *Son of God*, as Dr. Kendrick has pointed out, "was gloriously confirmed to Him when in His resurrection and ascension He was constituted *Son of God* in power" (cf. Rom 1:4).[7] It is indeed true that Jesus Christ was truly God's Son in a way that had no parallel. But even this does not seem to be "the name which is above every name" that completes and crowns all the others.

There are some others who point to the statement in Philippians 2:11 and say that the name is *Lord Jesus Christ*. This is a cogent suggestion, and has much to commend it. In all probability, it is nearer to the truth than any of the other suggestions because it includes the title *Lord* (*Kurios*) with the Messianic title, *Christ*, and the name of His humanity, *Jesus*. After the earthly redemptive work was accomplished, and following His resurrection, His divine nature fully vindicated, He was ready to take His deity and humanity together

7. A. C. Kendrick, *The Moral Conflict of Humanity and Other Papers*, pp. 80-81.

to the throne of supreme dominion and universal headship, and exercise all the functions of *Lord over all.*

This points to the name which seems most to qualify as "the name which is above every name"—the name *Jehovah,* that name unique and glorious, which the Jews would not utter. This is the name supreme, the "I AM" who exists eternal and unchangeable, who will always be what He will be: infinite, eternal, personal, perpetual, absolute. This is the name that stands above all the others, and which seems to be the one intended here.

Kendrick says,

> This is clearly the title to which the apostle here has reference. This alone fits the description, "the name which is above every name," a description which the *heart* of the believer applies indeed to "Jesus," but not in the sense here had in view by the apostle. The apostle's reference here is evidently objective, not subjective; it refers to a name intrinsically significant of pre-eminent exaltation, a name which God *bestowed, conferred* upon Him as a mark of favor, and which accompanied His elevation. "Jesus" was the name of His lowliness; it was given, not conferred; it marked service, not rank; it was brought with Him to His heavenly throne, not received there. I emphasize the use of the verb "bestowed, conferred," which is not appropriate to the name "Jesus." All this points to the name "Lord" except the position of the Name "Jesus." But to a closer observation this bears the same testimony. He who had borne this name on earth is to be vindicated in heaven, and for this the name (not a name) which transcends every other is conferred upon Him, that every tongue in heaven, earth, and hades, may acknowledge His *Lordship.* The apostle skillfully prepares the way for this climax of his thought. . . . The word "Lord" becomes the apex of an inverted pyramid, defining and concentrating the swelling thought which is held back till it bursts its boundaries of expression. Let the reader read thoughtfully the sentence as a whole, and doubt, if he can,

that the name "Lord" was that which God conferred upon Jesus when He highly exalted Him.[8]

The following reasons support this conclusion:

1. The name Jehovah is the name most fitting when compared carefully with the word Lord (Gr., *Kurios*) in verse 11. The term *Lord* stands in the Scriptures as the New Testament equivalent of the Old Testament name *Jehovah,* and occurs repeatedly in the Septuagint, where the word *Jehovah* would appear for *Lord.*

2. The name Jehovah was the ineffable name of the living God among the Hebrews. Hence, it is the one great name by which it is to be expected that Christ, the Lord, would be recognized and acknowledged.

3. The name of His humiliation is Jesus, whereas the name of His exaltation is Lord. The two are placed in marked antithesis to each other. Every knee shall bow in worship of the Man Jesus, born in Bethlehem, who died on a cross for our sins. As the Man Jesus, He will command the worship and obeisance of every being in the universe. But all shall unite in owning Jesus the Man to be Lord of all. That name which is above every name that is named, including His own human name *Jesus,* can only be the great name *Jehovah.*

This name of verse 9 is given to Him *because of His humiliation,* in view of the fact that He humbled Himself (see John 5:27). Thus it cannot be the name of His humiliation. The explanation cannot be that because Christ humbled Himself to become "Jesus," God the Father gave Him *the same name* in His exaltation, but with a new majesty and nobility attached to it. That ignores the testimony of verses 10 and 11, and the use of the name "Lord." The confession which the apostle urges that unbelievers must make when they receive Him as their Saviour is the confession of Jesus *as Lord:* "If thou shalt confess with thy mouth *Jesus as Lord,* and shalt

8. Ibid., pp. 82-83.

believe in thine heart that God hath raised him from the dead, thou shalt be saved" (Rom 10:9, author's trans.). The confession of the Man Christ Jesus *as Lord* is the very essence of the gospel. And when the apostle declares the essential content of his preaching and that of his fellow servants, he says: "For we preach not ourselves, but Christ Jesus *the Lord*" (2 Cor 4:5, italics added). The name cannot be other than the great name *Jehovah.*

4. The name Jehovah is the specific and particular designation of the God of revelation. Whenever God desired to give to His people a special revelation of Himself, He used the name *Jehovah.* As Jehovah He expressed Himself in His essential moral and spiritual attributes to His covenant people, Israel.

In Exodus 3:14-15, it is recorded that God spoke to Moses, identifying Himself as "I AM THAT I AM." This title has the same root as the name *Jehovah.* The name *Jehovah,* as it appears in Exodus 6:3 (Heb., *Yehowah*), is derived from the Hebrew "I AM" (*havah*) in Exodus 3:14-15. When our Lord Jesus Christ appeared in His public ministry, He used the specific formula "I am" (Gr., *egō eimi*) of Himself, as John records more than twenty times in the fourth gospel, thus identifying Himself as the "I AM" of Exodus.[9]

5. The name Jehovah is the designation for the God of redemption. The true significance of this name was unfolded by the manifestation of God as a personal, living being in the incarnation, in the full revelation of His redeeming mercy, for He came into the world, in fulfillment of the words of the prophet Isaiah, to save His people from their sins (Matt 1:21). Revealing Himself to Israel through *the written Word* and through flesh, *the living Word,* He is Jehovah, the God of revelation, who appeared for man's redemption. He is the permanent and unchangeable One: in the Old Testament,

9. See John 6:35; 8:12; 8:23, 24, 28; 10:7; 11:25; 15:1.

The Exaltation of Christ   133

"I [am] Jehovah, [I] change not" (Mal 3:6, ASV); and in the New Testament, "Jesus Christ the same yesterday, and to day, and for ever" (Heb 13:8). This revelation of Himself is never with the signature "Thus saith *God* [*Elohim*]," but always "Thus saith the LORD [*Jehovah*]," the New Testament *Kurios*.

This is the name that transcends every other name. This is the name that is conferred upon our blessed Lord, so that every tongue in heaven, earth, and hades—in all the universe— will acknowledge His supreme and absolute lordship.

THE RECOGNITION OF CHRIST'S UNIVERSAL SOVEREIGNTY

THE GROUND OF THE RECOGNITION

The purpose of the exaltation, for which God has given Christ this name above every name, that "at the name of Jesus every knee should bow" (Phil 2:10). The prepositional phrase "at [lit., "in"] the name of Jesus" immediately follows the word "that" and stands emphatically at the beginning of the sentence. It marks out *the ground,* or occasion, of the bowing of every knee. The statement is based upon the great prophecy of Isaiah 45:20-23, which announces the future universal worship and adoration of the Lord of glory. The name is the name which has been conferred upon the Son of God, the name "Jehovah," which appears in verse 21 (ASV) of the prophecy: "Who hath showed this. . . . Have not I, Jehovah?" The phrase "name of Jesus" does not properly refer to the name *Jesus,* as some insist; it is a possessive genitive construction in the original Greek text and so denotes *the name which belongs to Jesus.* The whole context decides the matter, and the name in which every knee bows is the name established in verse 9, "Jehovah," which belongs to Jesus. "Every knee shall bow" is indicative of universal veneration, not worship *through* the name but homage given *to the One* who bears that name.

THE GREATNESS OF THE RECOGNITION

The recognition is universal. While the word "creature" is the neuter term for "created things" (cf. 1 Tim 4:4), it is also descriptive of personal "beings," as is evident from James 1:18. In Revelation 5:13, the worship of all the redeemed and the host of angels seems to be included in the description of the utterance of all created things. The praise and adoration rise from all quarters of the universe, and to limit this worship to either rational or animate creation is to deprive the passage of its fullness and universal scope. In Revelation 4:11, the Lord of creation is glorified because of His creative work in calling every created thing into existence, "Thou art worthy, O Lord, to receive glory and honour and power: for thou hast created all things." In Revelation 5:13, all the created things in the universe are seen glorifying the One on the heavenly throne. The book of Psalms describes every created thing, animate and inanimate, as joining in the praise to the Lord of the universe (Psalm 148). Mountains, hills, fruitful trees, cedars, beasts, cattle, creeping things and flying fowls, sun and moon, as well as the kings of the earth, and all peoples, are called upon to bless the name of the Lord.

The apostle Paul portrays all creation as waiting in eager anticipation for full redemption, the redemption of the body (Rom 8:23), and looks forward to the time when the whole creation will bend the knee in homage, worship, and praise to the Lord of glory (Rom 8:19-23; Phil 2:10). The entire universe and everything in it will unite in rendering praise, honor, and glory to the Lamb of God. All shall bow in submission and subjection to Jehovah, the Lord of heaven and earth, and acknowledge Him as Sovereign.

In these days, all knees do not bow to His name, and many hearts are not humbled. Man's worship is often not honorable or becoming to the Lord Jesus Christ. Certainly much of it is not in spirit and in truth, and many flatly refuse to worship

Him. There is an apostasy which paints the name "Jesus" on its banners, and flaunts them about, publishing Him as the best and greatest of mankind, and the revolutionary of the hour. There is also an apostasy which deliberately denies Christ, and disavows His claim to deity and authority. Both alike are opposed to Him. This mass apostasy is rapidly gathering volume and force, and already is worldwide in scope. And in these days when the gospel of a "Jesus" who is mere man, who simply died as any other man, yet who left behind Him a noble example and a spirit and attitude which pervade all men, the witness of true Christians should be marked by a clear confession of Christ as Jehovah, the Most High God, who rules in the world of men. In the face of easy familiarity in the use of the name "Jesus," which is so common today, we must give proof by our walk and words that we know Him and own Him as *Lord,* the Lord of glory, the Jehovah of the Old Testament. There is but one Lord Jesus Christ, and He is the Saviour of our souls, the Son of God, the King of kings and Lord of lords.

Someday we shall see Him as He is, and we shall bow the knee in His presence, for not even the holiest of mortal men can stand before the glory of the Lord God Almighty. This high regard for the unique and blessed person of our Lord Jesus Christ was once expressed by Charles Lamb in conversation with some of his friends: "If Shakespeare was to come into this room, we should applaud him; if Abraham Lincoln entered the room, we should all rise to honor him; but if Jesus Christ was to come into it, we should all fall down upon our faces."[10]

The Rendition of Universal Homage to Christ as Lord

Verse 11 is the great climax of the passage, which moves from the humiliation of the Saviour to the homage rendered

10. Charles Lamb, quoted in D. Mial Edwards, *The Lord of Life,* p. 231.

to the Lord of glory. Exaltation follows on self-abasement, glory on humility. Our Lord Jesus Christ will receive the homage of the universe. Even His enemies will be constrained to bow to His authority and submit to His holy will. He will then stand forth as King of kings and Lord of lords, but not because He sought His own exaltation and glory, not even after His humiliation. "*God* . . . highly exalted him" (Phil 2:9, italics added).

HOMAGE EXPRESSED BY UNIVERSAL CONFESSION

The first clause of verse 11 reads: "And that every tongue should confess." As we have seen, this statement is based upon the great passage in Isaiah 45:23. The verb "confess" means "to speak out in full, openly, joyfully," or simply "to speak out plainly and publicly in the presence of others."

The first usage is the predominant one, as all the sources show. This indicates the nature of the great confession on the part of the saved. It describes the acknowledgment, homage, adoration, and worship which will break forth out of the hearts of all believers as they confess themselves to Christ. Wiesinger says, "What the bending of the knee indicates [v. 10], the tongue expresses."[11]

But *every* knee shall bow, *all* classes shall engage in this confession. It is universal in scope. Of all classes of mankind, not one knee shall be unbent, not one tongue will be unused in this confession. It is suggested by some writers that the exalted honor paid to the Saviour, and the universal acknowledgment of His lordship are offered gladly and heartily by the redeemed, but that those who have not believed will do so, yet with fear, by compulsion, against their will. However, to speak of involuntary adoration and a forced confession on the part of some is to mar the language and contradict the purpose of the confession. The point here is that when the Lord

11. Wiesinger, as quoted by Braune, "Philippians," in Lange's *Commentary on the Holy Scriptures*, 21:36.

stands forth in all His glory, none will be able to deny the lordship and power of the God-man, Jesus Christ. This is a confession of absolute deity, the final and universal acknowledgment of Christ's sovereignty. Jesus the historical Person, the human Servant, the Saviour and Anointed One, Christ, is sole and absolute Sovereign, Lord over all. The One who came down from heaven and entered the human race by virgin birth and incarnation so long ago, and who hung on the cross accursed, in our place, in His human nature, is the Lord of glory. And, as Lenski remarks, "All the universe will not only see it, but see it so that the confession and the acknowledgment of it cannot, will not, be with-held."[12]

All the hosts of heaven and all the human race who still live, have lived, or shall live, and all under the earth, will bend the knee before Him, and will confess openly and plainly that He is *Lord over all the universe.* All who never received Him, even those who denied and rejected Him, who opposed Him, and who were the enemies of the gospel, will then bow their knees in homage and plainly and fully confess His sovereign majesty and authority, unable to do other than to openly acknowledge who and what He is. The supreme triumph of His self-forgetfulness and sacrifice for others is embodied in the confessed sovereignty of the Saviour. He is the One who, as John testifies in Revelation 19:16, bears the title written on His vesture and thigh, "KING OF KINGS, AND LORD OF LORDS." Let us lay these words profoundly to heart, and allow the language, in all its wondrous majesty, to have its due weight and influence in our minds, and to be reflected in our lives.

The lesson to be learned is that the disciple is as His Master, the servant as his Lord. The witness of Christ, in a real sense, is to repeat itself in each who is His. We share His humiliation, His cross, His glory, His throne. We are crucified with

12. Lenski, p. 800.

Christ, so we must imitate Him in His humbling, emptying ourselves of pride and self-indulgence. We must deny ourselves, consider the things of others, and crucify the flesh with its affections and lusts, dying daily to the world and its things. So then we shall rise with Him now, in time, to newness of life and obedience in the daily walk. Afterward, we shall behold Him in His glory, and we shall be like Him, for we shall see Him as He is and shall sit with Him on His throne. "He that shall humble himself shall be exalted." Self-abasement must come first, then the glory; first the cross, and then the crown.

HOMAGE EXPRESSED FOR THE GLORY OF GOD

Philippians 2:11 ends with the words "to the glory of God the Father." The confession of the Son as Lord supreme is praise offered to the Father (see Ephesians 1:6, 12, 14). The glory of God the Father, from whom the whole plan of redemption proceeds, is the ultimate object of the Lord's incarnation and exaltation: "That God may be all in all" (1 Cor 15:28). That such should be the climax of the divine plan is right and proper, for what is this but compensation to the Father? The Father, during this present age of the church, has set Himself to glorify not Himself, but His self-sacrificing other self, the Son. He Himself thus exemplifies the self-forgetfulness and self-sacrifice which is the heart of the gospel. The Father is not looking on His own things any more than is the Son. Each Person of the great Trinity looks away from self to secure the glory of the Others. It is right in such circumstances that the glory of the Father should result from the consideration for others which He has shown, and that the mediatorial glory of the Son should be laid at the Father's feet. "For he that hath seen me [the Son] hath seen the Father" (John 14:9).

It must not be thought that God has been selfish in arranging all things for His own glory. When it is analyzed, we find that what might seem to superficial minds as a selfish arrangement is really absolute unselfishness. God has all along looked upon the things and interests of others, and has laid Himself out for their good. This has characterized the plan of God throughout its entire history; and when eventually the universe recognizes, acknowledges, and confesses the mighty self-forgetfulness of the eternal God, and this is hailed as the real glory, we cannot desire it otherwise.

We live in days that are fraught with danger and the deterioration of spiritual life. Apostasy is mounting rapidly, an apostasy of religious infidelity, which denies the whole doctrine of Christ. False sects and devil-worshipers, once afraid to make their identity public, now cry out for recognition and attention. Liberal theologians call such doctrines as the virgin birth of Christ, His deity, and His second coming trifling anachronisms. Religion is said to be a part of life, one more element along with vocation, family, recreation, and all the other things to which man gives himself. We can take it or leave it, depending upon how we feel about it. Scorn and opposition are increasing against those who witness a good confession of Jesus Christ. We must take heed and summon all our energy, courage, and determination to stand against the enemies of the gospel and against the evils that are gathering volume and force. For the truth is, the Saviour whom they deny, treading under foot the Son of God, doing despite to the Spirit of grace, is the One who is "over all, God blessed for ever" (Rom 9:5), and whose return to earth is imminent. The words of Robert Anderson are indeed appropriate in conclusion:

> It would seem, therefore, that even if we could find a scriptural warrant—*and I can find none*—for liberty to name the Lord of glory with the easy familiarity so common in these days, we should do well to forego that liberty, and to give proof by our very words, in season and out of season, that we are of the number of those who own Him as Lord, and

who honor Him "even as they honor the Father." The confession of Him thus as Lord is the very essence of the Gospel. "For if thou shalt confess with thy mouth Jesus *as Lord,* and shalt believe in thine heart that God hath raised Him from the dead, thou shalt be saved." But the god of this world has blinded the minds of the unbelieving, that the light of the Gospel of the glory of Christ, who is the image of God, should not shine unto them. The Gospel of a Jesus who is the image of man is Satan's chief device to delude his votaries today. But "we preach Christ Jesus as *Lord,*" the Apostle immediately adds (2 Cor. 4:4-5); and this the Devil cannot tolerate, for it impugns the lie of which he is the father—the lie that he himself is the true "firstborn," to whom the sovereignty of the world by right belongs. . . . "But ye call Me *Master and Lord,* and ye say well, for *so I am.*" These are the Lord's own words, and surely this is enough for every true disciple.[13]

> Safe in Jehovah's keeping,
>   Led by His glorious arm,
> God is Himself my refuge,
>   A present help from harm,
> Fears may at times distress me,
>   Griefs may my soul annoy,
> God is my strength and portion,
>   God my exceeding joy.
>
> Safe in Jehovah's keeping,
>   Safe in temptation's hour,
> Safe in the midst of perils,
>   Kept by almighty power,
> Safe when the tempest rages,
>   Safe though the night be long,
> E'en when the sky is darkest,
>   God is my strength and song.
>
> Sure is Jehovah's promise,
>   Nought can my hope assail,

13. Sir Robert Anderson, *The Lord from Heaven,* p. 95.

Here is my soul's sure anchor,
  Entered within the veil,
Blest in His love eternal,
  What can I want beside!
Safe through the blood that cleanseth,
  Safe in the Christ that died.

SIR ROBERT ANDERSON

ADDITIONAL NOTES

1. The false theories and misconceptions of the kenosis may be summarized in the following manner:

a. Christ's deity was veiled, and limited only in certain important respects.
b. Christ actually limited Himself, so His self-limitation was real, but inconsiderable.
c. Christ was in possession of all His attributes, but acted as though He was not.
d. He gave up certain relative attributes such as His omnipotence, omnipresence, and omniscience.
e. He did give up His essential attributes.
f. He emptied out of Himself all of His attributes, so that His deity was nonexistent.
g. The entire event took place merely in the earthly life of Christ.

These views have been refuted in the exposition of the passage.

2. The great central problem of the incarnation is the fact of the two natures in the one person of the Lord, and the relation of the divine to the human in the historic Christ. Paul makes no attempt to solve this problem in the Philippians text, and for the most part, the writers of the inspired Scriptures attest the reality of the two natures in the person of Christ without attempting to explain the matter. McClain comments:

> Perhaps it is wisdom to leave the matter as they have left it. One hesitates to enter a field of errors ranging from an Apollinarian denial of any human soul in the Saviour to the Nominalistic doctrine of two wills and two minds—in fact, two persons. But the Church has been compelled to enter this field by reason of the deviations of those who often-times were numbered among her own sons. At Chalcedon (A.D. 451) the Church declared that in the Saviour there were two natures, one divine and the other human. These two natures are perfectly and organically united

142

in one person, yet they remain distinct, each retaining its own complete integrity. We must neither confound the natures, nor divide the person. The seat of personality in the person is the Logos, the eternal Son.[1]

3. There is but one definite article occurring in the entire paragraph of verses 5 through 8, all the nouns being *anarthrous* (without the definite article). The single definite article in the text standing with the infinitive *einai* ("to be") is the only instance where the article appears. This item of Greek grammar indicates that the stress of the passage is upon *character, kind, quality,* and adds significantly to its exceptional doctrinal force and value. As to *character and essence,* Christ is true God, coeternal and coequal with God the Father. He is at the same time, by virtue of the virgin birth and incarnation, true Man, having taken upon Him the form of a servant. As to *character,* the death of a cross is infinite, affecting the whole universe; is all-sufficient, involving a ransom price paid in full; and final, being a finished work to which nothing can be added. As to *quality,* the humiliation of Christ was perfect, in that it consisted in the abdication of certain rights, involved the surrender of the independent exercise of sovereign powers, was a submission to servitude, and may be described as a descent to degradation and death.

4. The natural interpretation of the words "He emptied Himself" (*heauton ekenōsen*) and to which the facts point, is not that Christ put aside His divine nature. But He did divest Himself of the *form* which would, of itself, lead those who beheld that form to be sure that He possessed the divine nature. In emptying Himself, He laid aside the independent exercise of the divine attributes by which the form of God expressed itself. He assumed human flesh, form, and nature in the virgin birth and incarnation. The self-emptying brought about a change of *state*—the form of a slave for the form of God—but He did not divest Himself of His deity in the change. And in His human form, He retained the possession of deity, but He never manifested His deity apart from the will of the Father.

5. It should be pointed out, despite previous general reference

1. Alva J. McClain, "The Doctrine of the Kenosis in Philippians 2:5-8," *The Biblical Review* 13 (October 1928).

to this matter, that to the pronoun "who," with which verse 6 begins, Paul adds the words that follow in verses 6 through 11, *the whole summary of the history of our Lord Jesus Christ,* including His prehuman state. These verses set forth the complete doctrine of Christ except for specific reference to the return of the Lord, which, however, is implied by His exaltation to the place of power and glory, from whence He will come again. Meyer remarks, "And the force of the *example,* which certainly *comes first to light* in the historical Christ, has at once . . . its highest, because divine . . . obligation from, just what is said in ver. 6 of His state *before* His human appearance."[2]

6. While the emphasis of this great Christological statement is essentially *doctrinal,* at the same time the *example* of Christ is presented here with a completeness found in no other passage in the Scriptures. Christ, preexistent in the form of God, did not seek His own things but those of others, resolving as He did to not grasp His God-equal existence selfishly for His own enrichment. He emptied Himself, becoming a man, and stooping even to the death of a cross. God has highly exalted Him now to authority, sovereignty, and the place of lordship. So we who belong to Him enter into glory with Him only through the same way. We must go down the same thoroughfare, in the same path of lowliness, self-denial, and submission to the will of God, in full obedience to His Word. The pattern which Christ left for us, the Christian standard for all ages is threefold: it is a life of surrender *to* Him; it is a life of self-forgetfulness *in* Him; it is a life of service *for* Him.

7. It is absolutely essential for believers in our time to hold fast the true scriptural position with regard to this great Christological passage, and to maintain the correct doctrinal viewpoint with respect to the person of Christ. An alarming overemphasis on the humanity of Christ is sweeping the land and mounting in popularity, which has resulted in a de-emphasis on the deity of Christ and a dangerous lowering of the Lord's divine personality in the minds of many Christians. It is vital that we hold to the true doctrinal and practical teaching of the passage in Philippians 2:5-11,

2. H. A. W. Meyer, *Critical and Exegetical Hand-Book to the Epistles to the Philippians and Colossians, and to Philemon,* p. 66.

and to de-emphasize neither the perpetual unchangeableness of the deity of the Son of God in itself (John 1:1, 18; 10:30), nor His real, loving, self-denying, and self-abasing entrance into human life by virgin birth and incarnation to die for sinners and share with them His own eternal life (John 1:14; 6:51; 10:11). Here in these verses (Phil 2:5-11) is the whole doctrine of Christ, and to deny a single point of it is to deny it all.

8. Having said all this, we come to the end of the commentary on the great passage before us. The unsurpassed dogmatic treasures of this wonderful paragraph have not been—can never be—exhausted, by any means, even when we have drawn from it so much that it says to us concerning the glory of our Lord Jesus Christ. These imperfect lines of comment must suffice, however. But let us not fail to see how this passage of profound doctrinal splendor speaks so straightforwardly to us with a moving, practical appeal to the heart and life. The apostle Paul pleads for a life of love and accurate knowledge that is discerning and which encompasses and endorses only those things that are excellent in nature and character. He appeals to his readers on several bases: our common partaking in Christ and in the Holy Spirit; the fellowship of His sufferings and the power of His resurrection; and our great citizenship in that heavenly commonwealth from where we must constantly be looking for our Saviour, the Lord Jesus Christ.

But there is one more plea to the people of God: *"Let this mind be in you."* Here is at once the model and motive for all believers. Nothing less than the "mind of the Head" must be the "mind of the members." Charged to the brim as this passage is with the doctrine of the person and work of our blessed Lord, it is nevertheless a tremendously moving appeal to Christians to divest themselves of self-assertiveness and self-interest, that they may be found looking upon the things of others, in lowliness of mind esteeming others better than themselves. For the Saviour did, in fact, think and act in this manner for His own. As Bishop Moule so appropriately puts it: "Without the facts, which are doctrine, we might have had abundant rhetoric in St. Paul's appeal for unselfishness and harmony; but where would have been the mighty lever for the affections and the will? Reason of reason, argument of ar-

guments—the LORD JESUS CHRIST!"[3] Nothing in the true
Christian faith lies outside Him. He is the sum and substance of
it all. His person and His work embody all its dogmatic teaching.
The Christian faith, the blessed gospel, is *Christ*—no less.

3. H. C. G. Moule, *Philippian Studies*, pp. 102-3.

QUESTIONS FOR STUDY AND DISCUSSION

THE PREEXISTENCE OF CHRIST

1. Does it matter whether we believe in the preexistence of Christ?
2. In what form was Christ preexistent in heaven?
3. If Christ existed prior to His virgin birth in Bethlehem, does the Old Testament reveal anything about Him in His preexistent state?
4. If He actually appears in Old Testament times, how is He revealed in the pages of the Old Testament?
5. How does the New Testament treat Christ's preexistence?
6. In what manner does the Lord Himself refer to His preexistence?
7. Is it possible to believe in the preexistence of Christ and not hold to His deity?
8. What are the practical values of believing in this doctrine?

THE DEITY OF CHRIST

1. How are Christ's preexistence and deity related?
2. What are some of the various views concerning Christ's deity?
3. If Christ is truly God, how do we explain the reality of His manhood?
4. Is it possible that Christ was deified by those who were His followers?
5. If Christ is God, why—according to Mark 6:5—was He unable to do any "mighty work" in His own country?
6. What was our Lord's own attitude toward His equality with God the Father? How does He Himself speak of it?
7. Is belief in the deity of Christ essential to our faith in Him as Saviour? Give reasons for your answer.

8. Give some proof texts from the epistles for the deity of Christ.
9. How may verification of our Lord's deity be found in history and in Christian experience?
10. What are some of the practical values of the deity of Christ?

The Incarnation of Christ

1. What does the term *incarnation* mean?
2. What was the method by which the incarnation was accomplished? What part does the virgin birth play in the act of incarnation?
3. What changes took place in the Lord's position and state in the act of incarnation?
4. If Christ was and is truly God, was there any change in His divine personality when He became man?
5. How does one resolve the question of the two natures, Godhead and manhood, in the one person of Christ?
6. Did Christ possess all the essential elements of a true human being?
7. What importance does the New Testament assign to the incarnation?
8. Did Christ retain His humanity in His ascension, and in what form does He now appear at the right hand of God?
9. List the purposes of the incarnation.
10. How is the incarnation of practical importance and value to believers?

The Crucifixion of Christ

1. What are some of the various interpretations of the death of Christ? How do the liberal theologians assess Christ's death?
2. What place does the death of Christ occupy in the Scriptures?
3. Name some of the terms under which the crucifixion of Christ is spoken of in the Scriptures.
4. How specifically does the Bible set forth the death of Christ as substitutionary atonement?
5. What was the nature of the death of Christ? What were the physical and spiritual aspects of the Lord's crucifixion?
6. How is the death of Christ related to the Law?

7. List some of the results of the crucifixion. What was accomplished by Christ's death in relation to believers and to the whole human race?

8. How is the death of Christ *final*? Show how the Bible describes this with regard to the Lord Himself, to the saved, and to the world.

9. What are some of the wrong attitudes toward the death of Christ as pointed out in the Scriptures?

10. How does the Lord's death affect and influence the Christian life? What relation to the daily moral life and experience of believers does it have?

THE EXALTATION OF CHRIST

1. Was the ascension of Christ a real historical event, or were the apostles the victims of overemotion and hallucination (as many liberal theologians assert), and as a result only *thought* they saw Christ go up into heaven? How may we refute such a view?

2. Do the Scriptures make any attempt to explain the nature of the ascension?

3. In what form did the Lord ascend into glory?

4. Make a list of the passages which refer specifically to the ascension.

5. How is the ascension related to the Lord's present ministry and work? Discuss the nature of the work of the risen, ascended Lord.

6. Name and discuss some of the practical values of the doctrine of the ascension.

7. What is the significance of the great picture of the ascended Lord Jesus Christ given in Revelation 1:12-18?

8. What is the "name which is above every name" set forth in Philippians 2:9?

9. When do the universal bowing of the knees and the confession of Christ as Lord take place?

10. In view of the vital, gripping appeal which this great passage lays upon our hearts and minds, what should be the nature of our response to it?

BIBLIOGRAPHY

COMMENTARIES

Alford, Henry. "Philippians." In *The Greek Testament*. London: Rivingtons, 1862. Vol. 3, *Galatians–Philemon*.

Anderson, Sir Robert. *The Lord from Heaven*. Wheaton, Ill.: Van Kampen, n.d.

Andrews, H. T., et al. *The Lord of Life: A Fresh Approach to the Incarnation*. New York: Macmillan, 1929.

Barnes, Albert. *Notes Explanatory and Practical, on the Epistles of Paul to the Ephesians, Philippians, and Colossians*. New York: Harper, 1852.

———. *Notes on the Second Epistle to the Corinthians*. New York: Amer. Book, Harper, 1889.

Barry, Alfred. "Philippians." In *Ellicott's Commentary on the Whole Bible*, edited by Charles J. Ellicott. Vol. 3. Grand Rapids: Zondervan, 1943.

Bloomfield, S. T. "Philippians." In *The Greek Testament, with English Notes*. Vol. 2. Philadelphia: Clark & Hesser, 1854.

Braune, Karl. "Philippians." In Lange's *Commentary on the Holy Scriptures*, translated and edited by Peter Schaff. Vol. 21, *Galatians, Ephesians, Philippians, Colossians*. Grand Rapids: Zondervan, n.d.

Bruce, A. B. *The Humiliation of Christ*. Grand Rapids: Eerdmans, 1955.

Caffin, B. C. *Philippians*. The Pulpit Commentary, vol. 47. New York: Funk & Wagnalls, 1944.

Craddock, Fred B. *The Pre-existence of Christ in the New Testament*. Nashville: Abingdon, 1968.

Davies, Richard N. *The Doctrine of the Trinity*. New York: Hunt & Eaton, 1891.

Edgar, R. M. *Philippians*. The Pulpit Commentary, vol. 47. New York: Funk & Wagnalls, 1944.

Edwards, D. Mial. *The Lord of Life.* New York: Macmillan, 1929.

Girdlestone, Robert Baker. *Synonyms of the Old Testament.* Grand Rapids: Eerdmans, 1956.

Gough-Pidge, J. B. *The Epistle to the Philippians.* In *An American Commentary on the New Testament.* Vol. 5. Philadelphia: Amer. Bapt. Pubn. Soc., 1896.

Harrison, Everett F. *Introduction to the New Testament.* Grand Rapids: Eerdmans, 1964.

Hayes, D. A. "Epistle to the Philippians." In *The International Standard Bible Encyclopaedia,* edited by James Orr. Vol. 4. Grand Rapids: Eerdmans, 1939.

Henry, Matthew. "Philippians." In *Matthew Henry's Commentary on the Whole Bible,* edited by Leslie F. Church. New York: Revell, n.d. Vol. 6, *Acts to Revelation.*

Hiebert, D. Edmond. *An Introduction to the Pauline Epistles.* Chicago: Moody, 1954.

Kendrick, A. C. *The Moral Conflict of Humanity and Other Papers.* Philadelphia: Amer. Bapt. Pubn. Soc., 1894.

Kennedy, H. A. A. "The Epistle to the Philippians." In *The Expositor's Greek Testament,* edited by W. Robertson Nicoll. Vol. 3. Grand Rapids: Eerdmans, n.d.

Lange, John Peter. *Commentary on the Holy Scriptures,* edited by Philip Schaff. Vol. 17, *The Gospel According to John,* translated by Edward Yeomans and Evelina Moore. Grand Rapids: Zondervan, 1945.

Lenski, R. C. H. *The Interpretation of St. Paul's Epistles to the Galatians, to the Ephesians, and to the Philippians.* Columbus: Lutheran Book Concern, 1937.

———. *The Interpretation of St. John's Gospel.* Columbus: Lutheran Book Concern, 1942.

———. *The Interpretation of St. John's Revelation.* Columbus: Wartburg, 1943.

Lightfoot, J. B. *Saint Paul's Epistle to the Philippians.* Grand Rapids: Zondervan, 1953.

Machen, J. Gresham. *The Virgin Birth of Christ.* New York: Harper, 1930.

McClain, Alva J. "The Doctrine of the Kenosis in Philippians 2:5-8," *The Biblical Review* 13 (October 1928).

Meyer, H. A. W. *Critical and Exegetical Hand-Book to the Epistles to the Philippians and Colossians, and to Philemon.* New York: Funk & Wagnalls, 1885.

Morgan, G. Campbell. *The Crises of the Christ.* New York: Revell, 1936.

Moule, H. C. G. *Philippian Studies.* London: Pickering & Inglis, n.d.

Niesel, Wilhelm. *The Theology of Calvin.* Philadelphia: Westminster, 1956.

Rainy, Robert. "The Epistle to the Philippians." In *The Expositor's Bible.* Vol. 6. Grand Rapids: Eerdmans, 1940.

Ryrie, Charles C. *Biblical Theology of the New Testament.* Chicago: Moody, 1959.

Seiss, Joseph A. *The Apocalypse: Lectures on the Book of Revelation.* Grand Rapids: Zondervan, n.d.

Shedd, William. *Dogmatic Theology.* 3 vols. New York: Scribner, 1889.

Simpson, P. C. *The Fact of Christ.* New York: Revell, n.d.

Speer, Robert E. "God in Christ the Only Revelation of the Fatherhood of God." In *The Fundamentals.* Vol. 2. Los Angeles: BIOLA, 1917.

Stock, John. "The God-Man." In *The Fundamentals.* Vol. 2. Los Angeles: BIOLA, 1917.

Strong, A. H. *Systematic Theology.* Philadelphia: Judson, 1907.

Tenney, Merrill C. *The New Testament, An Historical and Analytical Survey.* Grand Rapids: Eerdmans, 1953.

Thiessen, Henry C. *Introduction to the New Testament.* 3d ed. Grand Rapids: Eerdmans, 1955.

Torrey, R. A. *What the Bible Teaches.* New York: Revell, 1933.

Vincent, Marvin R. *The Epistles of Paul.* In *Word Studies in the New Testament.* Vol. 3. Grand Rapids: Eerdmans, 1946.

Warfield, Benjamin B. "The Deity of Christ." In *The Fundamentals.* Vol. 2. Los Angeles: BIOLA, 1917.

Weston, Henry G. *An Outline of Systematic Theology.* Philadelphia: Amer. Bapt. Pubn. Soc., 1895.

Wuest, Kenneth S. *Philippians in the Greek New Testament.* Grand Rapids: Eerdmans, 1944.

LEXICONS, CONCORDANCES, AND DICTIONARIES

Arndt, William F., and Gingrich, F. Wilbur. *A Greek-English Lexicon of the New Testament.* Chicago: U. Chicago, 1957.

Cremer, Hermann. *A Biblio-Theological Lexicon of New Testament Greek.* 4th ed. Reprint. Edinburgh: T. & T. Clark, 1954.

Davidson, Benjamin. *Analytical Hebrew and Chaldee Lexicon of the Old Testament.* MacDill AFB, Fla.: MacDonald, n.d.

Green, Samuel G. *Handbook to the Grammar of the Greek New Testament.* New York: Revell, n.d.

Harkavy, A. *Students Hebrew and Chaldee Dictionary.* New York: Hebrew Pub., 1918.

Lampe, G. W. H., ed. *Patristic Greek Lexicon.* Oxford: Clarendon, 1961.

Liddell, Henry George, and Scott, Robert. *A Greek-English Lexicon.* New York: Harper, 1870.

Moulton, James Hope, and Milligan, George. *The Vocabulary of the Greek New Testament.* Grand Rapids: Eerdmans, 1949.

Orr, James, ed. *International Standard Bible Encyclopaedia.* 5 vols. Grand Rapids: Eerdmans, 1939.

Pick, Aaron. *The English and Hebrew Bible Student's Concordance.* Prague: Bible Study Classic, n.d.

Pickering, John. *A Comprehensive Lexicon of the Greek Language.* Rev. ed. Philadelphia: Lippincott, 1889.

Robinson, Edward. *A Greek and English Lexicon of the New Testament.* London: Longman, Orme, Brown, Green, & Longmans, 1937.

Thayer, Joseph H. *A Greek-English Lexicon of the New Testament.* Corrected ed. New York: Amer. Book, 1889.

TEXTS

Codex, Alexandrinus. Reduced Photographic Facsimile. *The New Testament and Clementine Epistles.* London: Longmans, 1909.

Kittel, R. *Biblia Hebraica.* New York: Amer. Bible Soc., n.d.

Nestle, E. *The New Testament Greek Text.* London: British & Foreign Bible Soc., 1939.

Textus Receptus, The. The Greek text underlying the English Authorized Version of 1611. London: Trinitarian Bible Soc., 1976.

Westcott, B. F., and Hort, F. J. A. *The New Testament in the Original Greek.* New York: Macmillan, 1940.

Bible Versions

The New Scofield Reference Bible. New York: Oxford U., 1967.
The Revised Standard Version of 1901. New York: Nelson, 1929.
The Septuagint Version. Edited by Alfred Rahlfs. New York: Amer. Bible Soc., 1952.

Grammars

Dana, H. E., and Mantey, Julius R. *A Manual Grammar of the Greek New Testament.* New York: Macmillan, 1948.
Goetchius, Eugene Van Ness. *The Language of the New Testament.* New York: Scribner, 1965.
Goodwin, William Watson. *Greek Grammar.* New York: Ginn, 1930.
Huddilston, John Homer. *Essentials of New Testament Greek.* New York: Macmillan, 1931.
Robertson, A. T. *A Grammar of the Greek New Testament in the Light of Historical Research.* New York: Doran, 1915.

Miscellaneous Sources

Darby, J. N. "Philippians." In *Synopsis of the Books of the Bible.* London: Cooper & Budd, 1949. Vol. 4, *Acts—Philippians.*
Easton, Burton Scott. "The Kenosis," in *International Standard Bible Encyclopaedia.* Vol. 3. Grand Rapids: Eerdmans, 1939.
Hodge, Archibald Alexander. *A Commentary on the Confession of Faith.* Philadelphia: Presbyterian Board of Educ., 1869.
Moule, C. F. D. *An Idiom-Book of New Testament Greek.* Cambridge: U. Press, 1963.
Orr, James. "The Virgin Birth of Christ." In *The Fundamentals.* Vol. 2. Los Angeles: BIOLA, 1917.
Stone, Nathan J. *Names of God.* Chicago: Moody, 1944.
Tucker, Joshua T. *The Sinless One, or The Life Manifested.* Boston: Whipple, 1855.